THE ART OF
Diana Armfield

THE ART OF

Diana Armfield

JULIAN HALSBY

David & Charles

ACKNOWLEDGEMENTS

We would like to have acknowledged individual ownership of all the works reproduced in this book, but as their whereabouts in many cases is unknown, and as nowadays many collectors prefer to remain anonymous, we can only gratefully acknowledge in a general way. We would like to thank the many people who have helped us gather together photographs and transparencies or who have helped us with valuable comments and advice: HRH The Prince of Wales, Browse and Darby, Manya Igel, Dr Katherine Watson, John Brandler, Brian Sinfield, Andrew Kimpton, Reuters, Mercury Asset Management Plc, Michael Jodrell, Mary Yapp, Charles Belloc-Lowndes, John Drummond, B. G. Salisbury and Arthur Ballard. We also acknowledge with thanks the following photographers: Helen Muspratt, Miki Slingsby, Matt Pia, John Jones, Roy Fox, Clive Boursnell, Leslie MacIntyre and Nigel Cheffers. Catherine Horwood, Miranda Halsby, Ken Howard RA and Bernard Dunstan RA all read the draft text and made useful comments and suggestions and all have been most encouraging throughout the writing of this book. To them and to our editor, Alison Elks, who helped bring this book about, we extend our warmest thanks.

(Page 2) ***Tall Vines below San Gimignano***
Oil, 13½ × 18in (34.3 × 45.7cm), 1991

'One of my favourite kinds of landscape; a blue distance, spotted slopes and in the foreground, blond soil between rows of luxuriant vine growth. The pollarded tree which supported the vines and marked the beginning of the row, carried two branches which displayed that open, generous gesture that comes in nature and is so much part of Turner's work. I did two versions of this landscape, a small panel on the site, and this larger one from the sketch and a supporting drawing.'

A DAVID & CHARLES BOOK

Copyright © text: Julian Halsby 1995
© illustrations: Diana Armfield 1995

First published 1995

Julian Halsby has asserted his right to be identified as author of this work in accordance with the Copyright, Designs and Patents Act 1988.

A catalogue record for this book is available from the British Library.

ISBN 0 7153 0233 7

Typeset by ABM Typographics Ltd, Hull
and printed in Singapore by C S Graphics Pte Ltd
for David & Charles
Brunel House   Newton Abbot   Devon

(Page 3) ***Kew in the Snow***
Oil, 7½ × 8¼in (19 × 21cm), 1991

Most of Diana's snow scenes are painted in Wales, and this work, painted near her house in Kew, is something of an exception. This is very much a tonal painting with the palette restricted to a close range of whites, greys and earth colours; contrast is provided by the black of the woman's coat, the red of her hat and the purple pinks of the child's clothes. The figures are more clearly delineated and their comparative sharpness is balanced in the composition by the form of the white bus stop sign.

CONTENTS

Camellias in a Winter Bunch on the Studio Table

Oil, 23½ × 18in (59.7 × 45.7cm), 1988–89

This splendid picture has all the richness, variety and intensity which make Diana Armfield's flower paintings among the finest in post-war British art. She achieves an almost baroque profusion of blooms and foliage which is held together by the rich pinks of the camellias grown in her garden in Kew. The artist talks of her practice of creating a framework – in this case the jug, the table and mounting boards behind – over which she then allows nature to spread in abundance. Notice the richness of paint in certain areas of the flowers and leaves, contrasted by the thinner use of paint allowing the colour of the toned panel to show through in the foreground. Notice also how the viewer's eye is held within the composition, being led back by the parallel lines on the table, up towards the camellias, out along the overflowing sprays of leaves and down towards the table. The artist enjoys the play of 'painted' flowers within a picture, in this case the decorations on the jug, and the 'real' flowers in the jug.

FOREWORD

Why is it that there are fewer women painters than men, indeed far fewer in any field of the arts than men? The answer is very simple: men, by tradition, fit their life around their work, and women fit work around their life. This, at first sight, may appear to be a weakness and yet I believe it to be a strength, for painters such as Diana Armfield pour their whole life into their work; theirs is a sensibility born of giving and born of being a wife and a mother as well as a creative artist.

I have known Diana's work over many years, first becoming familiar with it through the exhibitions of the New English Art Club. Diana is a worthy successor to such painters as Walter Sickert and Gwen John; the roots of her work are in France, and the New English Art Club was founded as a revolt against the academic standards of the day and as a celebration of the modern French tradition of Corot, Courbet, Degas and the Impressionists. Since those early days, the New English Tradition has survived and latterly flourished, again largely through the work of painters such as Diana Armfield.

Diana opens our eyes to the world, she shows it to us in her terms, she convinces us that the world she reveals to us is the world. A personal vision is the basis of all art; so as when we hear the music of a particular composer and immediately recognise his language, so too when we enter a mixed exhibition we immediately recognise the work of Diana Armfield. Here is a small, still voice that speaks to us quietly but persuasively. We have all witnessed each year how her work sings out at the Royal Academy of Arts Summer Exhibition, without the need for vast scale or strident colour, along with other New English painters such as the late Peter Greenham and Bernard Dunstan.

Like all exceptional painters, Diana Armfield stamps her identity on a subject, and by so doing becomes inextricably associated with it. She, without any doubt, has stamped her identity on the still life with flowers. Not for her the large vase of exotic blooms, she has made the wild flower, the informal flower, her own. This is in itself an achievement, for no subject in painting has been more overdone than the flower, no subject has been more badly painted than the flower. Yet Diana has returned to it its dignity, its simplicity, and has continued a worthy tradition of painting the subject that has continued from Fantin-Latour, through the Impressionists and such quiet English masters as the late Allen Gwynne-Jones.

It is a mark of Diana's achievement that she has always worked within a small format, indeed I cannot remember seeing a painting by her that was larger than 20 × 24 inches. This typifies her stubborn perseverance and determination to follow her own path regardless of the dictates of fashion and exhibition organisers. She has proven as clearly as any contemporary painter that scale has nothing to do with depth of expression. Diana says more in a panel of 10 × 12 inches than many painters manage on a canvas ten times as large.

Diana is a fine draughtswoman, a sure composer and an exquisite colourist. She has command of many ideas and is one of the finest pastellists living today. The true worth of her work was recognised three years ago when she was elected a Royal Academician. If a woman's life is her art, then this book celebrates what has been until now a rich and fulfilled life.

Ken Howard RA

1

FORMATIVE YEARS

Diana Armfield's grandfather, Joseph John, was a Londoner, born within the sound of Bow Bells. After an apprenticeship in a small Quaker engineering firm, he moved to Ringwood, Hampshire, where he bought a millwright's shop, transforming it over the following decades into a successful engineering works specializing in the manufacture of milling machinery. As a Quaker he believed in hard work, but he found time to act as a local Justice of the Peace, and to lecture at the working men's club. He married Josephine Margaret Maxwell, who came from a Scots family but grew up in Cornwall where she and her sister were known as the 'Belles of Penzance'. They established their home next to the engineering works. The River Avon ran at the bottom of their garden where they kept a rowing boat moored between the row of tall, black poplars, which every now and then dropped a bough on the lawn. The summer house where they kept their picnic paraphernalia escaped unscathed. The Armfields were a close, unworldly family, courteous and rather shy, but they attended concerts at the Bournemouth Pavilion and counted musicians amongst their close friends. Politics occupied quite a significant place in their lives – they supported the Liberal cause. They took their annual summer holidays on the Cornish coast, drawing and sketching the scenery and birds in watercolour.

Three children were born to the Armfields. The eldest, Maxwell Ashby Armfield RWS, 1882–1972, had no interest in the family firm. He studied at Birmingham School of Art and at the Atelier Colarossi in Paris. A slender man, rather fastidious, but with a liking for the theatrical, he wore a cloak while in Paris, and always dressed with a certain artistic flair. He was invariably short of money, but this rarely prevented him from spending extravagantly – a reaction perhaps to his Quaker background. Maxwell Armfield was to become one of the leading exponents of tempera painting in the twentieth century, and his work is represented in the Tate Gallery and in many public collections. He married Constance Smedley, an author and playwright. Constance was confined to a wheelchair, but was nevertheless an indefatigable organizer and a powerful personality. When her theatrical company, the Green Leaf Theatre, toured the United States, Maxwell designed the scenery and costumes for her productions.

The second child was a daughter, Margaret Daisy, who was never to marry, devoting herself entirely to her parents; she kept a journal which she illustrated with lively drawings and sketches. Joseph Harold, the youngest child, was Diana Armfield's father. Known to everyone as Harold, he studied engineering at Manchester University and took over the family business. An innovative and practical engineer, a 'contriver', he manufactured water turbines and the Hotchkiss cone propeller, spending many hours on the latter invention. Hotchkiss himself was rather eccentric and apparently drove his wife to distraction by expecting her to live in a house with nothing but curved walls. Diana has no aptitude for science or engineering, but thinks the attitude of a scientist and an artist has much in common, in spite of the different language.

Picnic tea by the River Avon, Heron Croft (Maxwell Armfield RWS) Tempera, 9¼ × 12¾in (23.5 × 32.4cm)

This painting shows Diana's grandparents with Daisy Armfield in the mid-1930s.

▷ *Interior of San Marco, Venice*
Pastel, 11 × 8½in (27.9 × 21.6cm), 1989

Diana discusses her experiences while drawing the interior of San Marco on page 96. Many artists have painted the façade of San Marco, but fewer have tackled its dark, mysterious interior, one exception being Sickert. A number of nineteenth-century artists made careful architectural studies of the interior, but in this pastel the artist captures the wonderful atmosphere inside the basilica.

◁ *Palladio wallpaper with four paintings*
Golden Stubble near St Félix (left)
6¼ × 8½in (15.8 × 21.6cm), 1983
'An oil sketch done on the way back to the hotel in the late afternoon sunshine, just a study in blue and gold in a favourite kind of landscape.'
Llanfor (top)
6 × 7½in (15.2 × 19cm), 1982
'A well-washed sky with great clouds crossing; a bright sky echoed by the black and white calves and cow in the field.'
The Barn, Majorca (bottom)
8¼ × 9in (21 × 22.9cm), 1980
'Above Estellencs, an intense blue sky making beautiful small shapes seen through the heavy scented foliage, the soil warm and rich.'
Below Volterra (right)
Oil, 6 × 7in (15.2 × 17.8cm), 1968
'One of my earliest paintings when I was looking for pattern.' (See page 33.)
The wallpaper, circa 1963
'The wallpaper had been designed in cut tissue paper and was produced by Palladio in three different colourways. Although a large repeat with quite separate shapes, I have enjoyed it as a background to pictures as all the shapes are flat and flow from one to another. It was based on ivy-leaved toadflax.'

▷ *At the Lapicques*
Pastel, 9 × 7in (22.9 × 17.8cm), 1989

'Enter past the concierge and up in the clattering lift to the 4th floor, out onto the narrow landing outside the Lapicque flat; one could only be in Paris. From the window of the little salon I could look down on the tops of the tall trees of the park across the Rue Froidevaux; inside the salon with its dusky pink walls hung a painting *Homage to Mozart* by Charles Lapicque, and from a later period in his career, a mobile sculpture occupied a corner of the room. Although there was an elegant faded couch in a smaller part of the room, meals and most conversation were at the table. Madame Aline Lapicque, herself a painter, sits opposite and her eldest son, Georges, on the right. Both carried on talking but sat very still to be drawn; the pastel was done later from the drawing and memory.'

◁ *Portrait of Diana Armfield* (Maxwell Armfield)
Tempera, 19¾ × 15¾in (50.2 × 40cm), 1942

'I enjoyed my several sittings for this portrait.
Maxwell was living in Glebe Place, off the King's
Road, Chelsea, and once through the door it was a
Maxwell interior; a mixture of primitive domestic
arrangements and interesting objects, books and
pictures. The sittings were largely taken up with
drawing, so I didn't see the painting in progress. I
had been doing wartime work in a smoke-float
factory and the dye in the powder had turned my
hair Venetian gold in colour. Maxwell was
enamoured with this and suggested that I dressed to
it with my gilt necklace and the rather sumptuous
jacket which he provided. The portfolio was there
to represent my future as a designer. We talked of
many things, and every now and then he followed
one of his rather abstruse comments with "I don't
suppose you are yet ready for that". I was mollified
by the word "yet". He gave me tea in exquisite,
carefully mended porcelain and had always made a
plateful of rather heavy biscuit-like cakes which
were quite delicious.'

'Both the artist and scientist have to have an intuitive grasp of a concept which is then developed by concentrated work and serious playing, called experiment! As a small child I often had to wait for my father in the machine shop, watching the milky oil and curling swarf coming off the machines, or in the foundry, wondering at the sight of the stream of molten metal. I think that I was only interested in the visual and dramatic aspect. Our own two eldest sons, Andrew and David, have inherited engineering and scientific gifts from both their grandfathers, Andrew being an engineer and inventor, and David a research physicist. Even our youngest son, Bob, a craftsman, can take an engine to pieces and put it together again.

'My father was practical; everything he made was built to last. Sometimes my mother had visualized beforehand something lighter and smaller, but she exercised great tact, and we still have several of his handsome pieces. Harold Armfield was tall, sweet-natured but very determined and largely silent – unless he had something to say, when he was often penetrating and even witty. He relied on my mother and her friends to provide much conversational entertainment. He was ardent in active pursuits, enjoying tennis, walking, and above all sailing. He kept a small, rather unseaworthy open boat, first at Christchurch and then at Poole. Later he bought the hull of an old lifeboat which he converted over the years into a cabin cruiser. It was eventually launched and he, with my mother and sister, sailed over to France.'

Diana's mother, Gertrude Mary Uttley, came from a large Lancashire family. Her father, a humorous but nervous man, owned a cotton firm in Manchester. She met Harold Armfield while she was studying Classics at Manchester University. Gertrude had great charm and could illuminate a topic for others both in conversation and in letters. Diana tells of her mother's interest in history and politics, distinctly left-wing. Gertrude

Armfield had found the rather Tory society of Ringwood, many of whom were retired from colonial service, difficult, but in time she made contact and many friends with the university socialists and Labour politicians from Southampton. While she was very reluctant to speak publicly, she was happy to organize political events, the most significant being in 1934 when she invited Victor Gollancz to address a meeting on the evils of Nazi Germany and in particular on the persecution of the Jews about which the audience had been largely ignorant or sceptical. Despite her political interests, Gertrude Armfield was at heart a romantic; she enjoyed the arts and the company of artists, and was delighted when, many years later, Diana married Bernard Dunstan.

In 1919 Harold and Gertrude Armfield moved into their

Oaktree House with Gertrude Armfield, taken some time during the 1940s.

Dusk in the Piazza, Venice
Pastel, 11¼ × 10¾in (28.5 × 27.3cm), 1987

'This was one of the very few occasions when I have been persuaded to leave well alone. Having worked my way down from the brilliant dusk-blue sky through the intricate front of San Marco to put one touch of a stronger blue of the sky on the child's jeans, I was just about to carry on with other touches on most of the other figures, when somebody came into the studio and said "Stop!". I did, apart from the pigeons and the few little accents of white to make a correspondence with the architectural division across San Marco.'

Christmas Rose on the Studio Table
Oil, 8 × 5¾in (20.3 × 14.6cm), 1971

On page 60 Diana describes how this was one of her
first oil paintings of flowers. The influence of her
training as a textile designer can be felt in the strong
sense of pattern in this painting. However, her
nascent interest in the textural qualities of leaves
and petals can be seen, as can her enjoyment of
decorated pottery.

The West Room at Oaktree House with Harold and Gertrude Armfield circa 1952 (showing fabrics by Diana Armfield; on one of the background walls is a small landscape by Bernard Dunstan).

new house, Oaktree, which he had designed. It had much in common with the Arts and Crafts Movement, the exterior having a traditional tiled roof, mellow red brick walls and visible woodwork in the windows and porches. The plan of the house was very modern for its time, with an almost open-plan ground floor, while the interior had polished wooden floors, off-white walls and wooden beams. Diana's room on the first floor had one window overlooking the garden with its beautiful cherry tree, and another looking across to the field where two goats were kept. The house was filled with paintings and prints, including a number of works by Maxwell Armfield and some etchings by Shannon.

'Most of the pictures round the house were originals, by friends or other relations besides Maxwell, but in my sister's bedroom hung a reproduction of the head of Botticelli's *Venus*, which I greatly admired for the coils and sweeps of her golden hair. When I was shown a reproduction of the whole work, I wondered much at the strange but beautiful distortion of the body. The painting still remains a favourite.'

Possibly of even greater importance for Diana was the garden, created from nearly four acres of open field by Gertrude Armfield. It consisted of a formal garden, kitchen garden, orchard, field, and 'The Scrub' which was overgrown with flowering gorse, bracken and young oak trees. 'Yew hedges helped to create a formal framework, a basic structure which looked good even in winter and against which plants and flowers brought colour and surprise in their season.' Diana often recalls that garden and suggests that it still has an influence on her thoughts as she composes her paintings.

Diana's older sister, Katherine Sylvia, known as Kay, was born in 1917. She was always considered the more 'intellectual' of the two girls and was given an academic education at Sidcot, a Quaker establishment, before joining Diana at Bedales for her last years at school. Diana was three years younger, born on 11 June 1920. As a child she spent much time writing stories and plays about animals and illustrating them, influenced at this stage by Beatrix Potter and Arthur Rackham, and it was evident to her parents that her interests lay in art, crafts, drama and music. In 1926, Maxwell Armfield and his wife, Constance, returned from the United States to a house called Mockbeggar, which they built with Harold Armfield's help, near Fordingbridge, Hampshire. There they staged dramatic productions, and Diana remembers being Cobweb in a performance of *A Midsummer Night's Dream*. After a period at a local dame-school, Diana was sent to board at Dunhurst, the junior school of Bedales, where crafts and music were taken seriously, and here she started to play the violin, taught by the Dolmetsch family.

HOLIDAYS AT L'ARCOUEST, BRITTANY

In 1929 the Armfield family spent the first of their annual holidays at L'Arcouest in Brittany. Diana speaks of the beauty of the bay at L'Arcouest, the pink rocks, the changing blues and greens of the sea, and deep golds of the seaweed. Three friends, Madame Curie of radium fame, Jean Perrin, a noted atomic physicist, and Charles Seignobos, a distinguished historian, had chosen this idyllic bay to build handsome houses in the local stone, so that their families and friends could stay there for the long summer vacations. The Armfields became attached to that group as 'the English friends'. Diana's parents and her sister Kay all spoke good French, and the family stayed with Charles Seignobos each summer. Most afternoons, after a memorable lunch, they sailed with him and his friends in his yacht *Eglantine*. They got to know the Lapicque family, daughter and son-in-law of Jean Perrin. Charles Lapicque had been a scientist, but changed direction to become a painter, achieving an international reputation. He spent many hours in his own boat absorbing the colour and shapes around him; later he would orchestrate them into his vibrant, high-key paintings. There were three boys in the family; the two elder, Georges and François, became lifelong friends. These friendships have endured, and years later Diana visited their father's memorial show in Paris, staying with his widow Aline, also a talented painter (see *At the Lapicques*, page 11).

Sometimes Diana forewent the sail to the islands, preferring to stay behind with the housekeeper Louise, to draw and make watercolour sketches of the flowers in the garden – dahlias, carnations, and blooms from a cascade of hydrangeas growing against the side of the house. On one occasion Madame Marot, a well-known textile designer whose marque is still widely available in Paris, came down the steps into the garden. She was dressed in a fabric of her own design, and Diana immediately decided that she too would become a textile designer. Diana feels that L'Arcouest has been an important influence, not only for the landscape but also for the friendships made there.

THE MACNAMARA FAMILY

Another friendship at this period was with the Macnamara family in Blashford, Ringwood.

'They were a lively family with three very beautiful, golden-haired girls, all painted many times by Augustus John. The two younger were rather wild, a family without a father at home. The eldest, Nicolette, graceful like her mother, later married the painter Anthony Devas RA, and after his death, Rupert Shephard NEAC. The next was Brigit and the youngest and wildest was Caitlin who married Dylan Thomas. They were older than us, but we sometimes spent the afternoon with them being thoroughly indulged, my mother retreating with their mother, Yvonne, into her charming sitting-room. Some years later my sister Kay and Caitlin were in Paris together. They met the sculptor Zadkine, and also the self-styled artists in Montparnasse; and after several months, Kay was "rescued" by her mother and brought home.'

BEDALES

After Dunhurst Diana went on to Bedales, which offered a broad education. 'We had good laboratories, a superb library and all of us took part in drama. Anyone learning an instrument played in the orchestra, which gave me, an indifferent performer, a privileged insight into music.' She found the division of the day into short periods difficult to tolerate, so found sanctuary at 'The Barn', the craft centre built two fields away. There she could immerse herself all afternoon when allowed, weaving or learning some other craft. An all-important influence was the eccentric art master, Innes Meo, known as 'Gigi'.

◁ *Roses in a Summer Bunch, Llwynhir*
Oil, 12¼ × 10⅖in (31.1 × 26.7cm), 1988

A simple composition dominated by the deep pink rose which grows in Diana's garden in Wales. She describes a dominant bloom in such a composition as the '*prima donna*' which dominates but needs to be supported by the smaller flowers on each side. Notice the rich blue shadow in the foreground and the broken brushwork which keeps the paint surface alive and fresh.

▷ *Christmas Flowers on the Piano*
Oil, 10½ × 12¼in (26.7 × 31.1cm), 1988–89

'There is particular pleasure to be had in the days around Christmas, searching round the Welsh garden to find enough blooms to make a bunch to paint; midwinter, yet a suggestion of spring. The little pansy with the dark yellow centre I thought perfect as a foil to the larger Christmas rose. The *Vibernum fragrans* was half lost against the polished wood of the piano, which itself was much modified by reflections.'

'Of Italian extraction, he had deep-set, penetrating eyes beneath undisciplined eyebrows. He was susceptible to all comely girls, but kept a mocking, watchful eye on the boys as they stepped over the threshold of the studio. Any that he took against he dispatched without appeal to the matron, with a note which read "This boy needs a rest". Having got rid of the unwanted, he turned to entertain and spellbind the rest of us with hair-raising stories of his "escapes" from the Germans during World War I. Given large sheets of cartridge paper and a piece of charcoal, we were then told to draw these scenes from our imagination. The remaining boys enjoyed this, but I found it virtually impossible, and usually got my own way to draw something from his abundant collection of still lifes or jugs of flowers, or quite often to take my board and paper out into the grounds to draw the landscape.

'Innes Meo was a good draughtsman, in the Slade tradition. I was in turn influenced and tried to copy his fluid line. Occasionally he took a few of us to Portsmouth docklands to see and draw what he called "real life", as he regarded us all as ignorant and privileged. He placed much greater emphasis on drawing than painting on the spot, saying, "With a fairly good drawing it's in the bag; with anything but a superb watercolour you've got nothing!" As art master he was responsible for the scenery of all stage productions. One afternoon he asked me to help him create a café scene; there were to be glasses on little tables. Most reluctantly, quite sure that I would be useless, I joined him on the stage, to be shown with one dexterous example what was wanted. To my delight my apparently crude and meaningless brush strokes became, from a little way off, glinting glasses. I drew and painted during the holidays, occasionally going off on a day's painting in Dorset or a few days in the Clun country. Accompanied by my cousin Nigel Tolson, later to become an architect, we stayed at youth hostels. I remember comparing my rather wayward efforts to his secure but witty architectural drawings and preferring his. I recall one

summer spending several hours painting a group of Michaelmas daisies on which alighted red admiral and peacock butterflies. It was an experience of true conscious bliss, perhaps the first connected with painting. It has repeated itself on occasions when working on the spot, throughout my painting life. It happens only when the work flows, the sun warms and there are suggestions of scent from herbs, flowers or fresh foliage.'

PARIS 1937

The regime at Bedales was somewhat spartan. Cold baths were insisted on every morning and parts of the building were draughty; Diana regularly succumbed to flu and rarely had a complete autumn or spring term at school. As a result, when she left school in 1937 she had failed her School Certificate in French and was sent to Paris for three months, spending part of the time with the Lapicques near Denfert-Rochereau. She attended an art atelier to draw the nude, and watched the progress of a mural by Charles Lapicque, but to her sorrow was too shy to help when asked. However, she accompanied Charles round old parts of Paris where pieces of old faience could be picked up for his collection, and she also became acquainted with all the major galleries of Impressionist and Post-Impressionist painting.

An old friend of her mother's felt responsible for introducing her to the Louvre.

'She was not an experienced "gallery goer" and expected both of us to look at every work. Her ankles became swollen and I felt faint with fatigue but, of course, I did get something from those visits and returned by myself time and again to look at Ingres' *La Source* and other favourites. Perhaps this experience helped me to find a way with gargantuan collections. I can sweep my eye along the walls and am prepared to come away having really only looked at and absorbed a handful of works.'

On her return to England she re-took the School Certificate and, as a celebration for passing, joined a group of teachers on a tour to the Soviet Union. As well as memories of the trip, she came back with a treasure, a book on Ukranian folk art; its vigour and inventive colour influenced her textile design for some time.

THE SLADE AT OXFORD

After a spell at Bournemouth School of Art, Diana started in the textile department of the Central School in London. The Central closed on the outbreak of World War II, and she applied to the Slade School which had been evacuated to the Ashmolean in Oxford. She attended an interview with Professor Randolph Schwabe at his house in Beaumont Street. Her mother, having accompanied her on the drive for the sake of the jaunt, was ushered into the dining-room with her; coffee and biscuits were produced and the portfolio placed on the large polished table. Professor Schwabe turned over the sheets of indifferent life drawings and the rather better plant drawings. Coming to a bold design based on a bloom of *Magnolia grandiflora*, he shut the portfolio and, calling out to her mother who was sitting by the window, said with the stammer that he developed when at all excited, 'She can c-c-come!'

Diana drove up to Oxford in the engineering firm's Austin 7 and stayed with friends on Hinksey Hill. For the first weeks at the Slade she drew each day from the antique in the Long Gallery before moving on to the Life class. The students in the Life class were taught by Schwabe, George Charlton and Albert Rutherston, who all taught in the traditional way with demonstration drawings at the edge of the students' paper. Allan Gwynne-Jones taught painting in the Head Room and she recalls his military manner which in later years became affectionately benign. Dr Philip Hendy gave Art History lectures, but Diana found his delivery irresistibly somnolent.

Amongst her fellow students were Elizabeth Aslin, later

to become a museum director and authority on the Arts and Crafts Movement, and Milein Cosman who later married the music critic Hans Keller. She met and made friends with Cyril Frankel, who became a noted film director. One student stood out, 'a particularly attractive young man with dark hair and glasses hiding expressive eyes – Bernard Dunstan'. Bernard lived in a flat above a fur shop in Saunders Passage, off Broad Street. Hinksey Hill had proved too far out, so Bernard searched out for her a room for 12s 6d a week above a sweet shop at 51 St Giles. When she returned in the autumn, she found he had painted on one wall a mural of sky and white clouds seen through a window. Diana had a few petrol coupons to spare, so they set off to see the Stanley Spencer murals at Burghclere. 'Stanley Spencer is not one of my favourite artists, but the vision of the piled-up white crosses shining out remains a revelation to me.' Two years were spent in Oxford. She thoroughly enjoyed her time there, but in retrospect thinks that having the freedom of the university, she learnt more about life, politics and people than art, not really getting the best out of the Slade itself.

In 1942, Diana decided to leave the Slade and devote herself to war work. She was sent by the Ministry of Supply to work at various YMCA hostels, organizing all

Diana Armfield and John Drummond as students at the Central School printing their fabrics, 1947

◁ *Conversation at Florian's, Venice*
Pastel, 8½ × 10in (21.6 × 25.4cm), 1993

Diana enjoys working in the dark, opulent and richly decorated interior of Florian's, one of the old cafés situated in the Piazza San Marco (see page 41). While not defining in detail the faces and expressions of her subjects, the artist has managed to hint at their characters and to suggest that they are all engrossed in a cross-table conversation. The underworked foreground with the tables and jugs, suggested rather than spelled out in factual detail, leads our eyes towards the group, while behind the buildings on the other side of the Piazza, catching the reflections from a blue sky, is contrasted the artificial light of the nineteenth-century lamps. Notice how the couple to the right, one in a dark suit, the other in pink, provide a foil to the lady in the energetically patterned coat and hat seated in the middle of the composition. The young girl on the left, the least clearly defined of the figures, is looking towards her friend and her glance leads our eyes back into the picture. This is a masterpiece of suggestion and understatement creating a superb atmosphere.

▷ *Ristorante il Giglio*
Watercolour, 6 × 8in (15.2 × 20.3cm), 1991

This is a small restaurant where Diana and Bernard occasionally eat after a day's work in Venice. The artist has exploited the freshness and lightness of the watercolour medium to create a work full of light. The aim of this watercolour is quite different from the pastel on the opposite page. Here the emphasis is upon the whiteness of the table-cloths and waiters' jackets set against the cheerfully patterned wallpaper behind, rather than the rich, sombre atmosphere of the interior of Florian's.

kinds of events and activities for factory workers and soldiers. She ventured to raise a choir and orchestra for a performance of *The Messiah*, and its unexpected success provided a new-found confidence.

THE CENTRAL SCHOOL OF ART

In 1945 Diana returned to the Central School, where her real art education began. 'There were six mature students in the Textile Department, and we had real enthusiasm

Design for wallpaper and fabric (designed with tissue paper), 1964

and a desire to learn.' Three of the tutors were to influence her development both as a textile designer and ultimately as a painter.

'Joan Batty, a practising textile designer, gave us exercises in solving problems of abstract pattern-making. These exercises we carried out within the strict limitation of putting into repeat one-inch square linocuts. It amazed us that such restricted means could result in such diverse and inventive solutions and that most were easily attributable to particular students. Subsequently as a professional designer I included some of these patterns in my portfolio, and they were taken up by wallpaper manufacturers, but I have also found the principles on which they were based invaluable to me as a painter.

'These exercises looked forward to the courses in "Basic Design", taught as if totally innovative in art colleges in the 1960s. Sadly I found that those Fine Art students felt it only applied to abstract painting and most seemed to forget what they had learnt when they entered the Life Room or went out to paint landscapes.

'Bernard Adeney was the Head of Department, a cultivated man, a sensitive painter and a member of the London Group. Adeney confirmed Joan Batty's teaching while helping us with our own large-scale designs. He made us aware of "leading lines" and rhythms which take the eye beyond the edge of the motif, also the need to set up implied movement. He led me to feel that my motifs of leaves and flowers on the paper were alive and needing as much consideration as the real thing. He once leaned over my board, and said "You will bruise that delicate form in your drawing if you let it push up against that hard edge". Hans Tisdall arrived on the scene briefly and opened our eyes to the interaction of one colour against another, not in theory but in practice. Pointing a finger at two adjacent colours in a design he remarked, "This one, a shade cooler, will allow the other to sing". This comment, and others from Bernard Adeney, have stayed with me as talismans.'

THE ARMFIELD–PASSANO PARTNERSHIP

Several students from those years have become significant designers, including Mary Oliver and Terence Conran. However, it was with fellow student Roy Passano that Diana, on leaving the Central, set up a design partnership. Kay Armfield was by now married to William Watson, an archaeologist and expert on oriental antiquities who was working at the British Museum and was later to become a trustee. They were living at 7 Lambolle Road, Belsize Park, where there was a large studio at the end of the garden, and Diana, who had been living in the studio while a student at the Central, now established the Armfield–Passano Partnership there. Her father lent £150 and built them a long table for silk screen printing.

'We soon established a reputation but led a hand-to-mouth existence. We had no business experience and even getting the material on which to print was sometimes a nightmare because of rationing. We bought cloth from dubious sources, wheedling out bales of wartime balloon silk from under the counter, coupon free. Sometimes we had to wash it in the small sink in the studio, and hang it on a line in the garden before we could use it; it invariably caught London smuts. One dodge was to buy architects' tracing linen, and wash the dressing out, but this was expensive.'

Despite the problems they held two exhibitions in a gallery in South Molton Street in 1947 and 1948 and from these obtained enough orders to keep going. The Victoria and Albert Museum purchased examples for their Permanent Collection. They also provided hangings for the Finnish Legation and printed hessian for the walls of an exhibition entitled *40,000 Years of Modern Art*. Possibly the greatest accolade came when they were invited to submit hangings for the 1951 Festival of Britain, and were made members of the Society of Industrial Artists. 'Roy Passano

Interior of San Marco, Venice, 1989
Drawing on Canson paper for the pastel reproduced on page 11.

◁ *Nasturtiums*
Oil, 8½ × 9¼in (21.6 × 23.5cm), 1992

'Pure brightly coloured nasturtiums are one of my favourite late September flowers. I relish their luscious quality, slightly damp acrid perfume and the way they spill over the path and climb vigorously if given the chance. Their nearly flat rounded leaves make a fine foil to the elegant blooms. I painted this in one long session, as we were to leave Llwynhir within the next few days.

'The rooms in the cottage have deep window-sills, so the light from outside doesn't reach very far. I nearly always put the electric light on. While there is still daylight, the cast shadows are filled with blue or blue-violet, but by the time I had done all I could, there was only a hint of influence from the light outside. This was painted on a deep honey-coloured ground, so worked with very solid touches.'

▷ *September Landscape below San Gimignano*
Oil, 15¾ × 17in (40 × 43.2cm), 1988

Diana has painted this particular view on a number of occasions, and regards the spot as a kind of open-air studio. It is near San Gimignano and has many things that she looks for in a landscape – vines, a distant landscape melting into rich blues, pale fields of corn, accents of greens in the trees, and some architectural elements for both scale and colour. It also has a balance between an ordered landscape and a sense of 'waywardness' which is particularly appealing to Diana. She is often attracted to landscapes where, within a firm structure, the vines, trees or flowers rampage across man-made order. The lively brush strokes and the freshness of the colours give this landscape an immediacy, energy and sense of movement as well as a real feeling of the heat of the day.

would arrive in the studio early, sometimes before we'd finished breakfast; an embarrassment.' They also employed a Finn, a Mr Smiltens, who helped them block print, stamping with his feet all day, for £4 a week. 'He said he couldn't live on this, but it didn't matter as he made his "real" money on the dogs.'

MARRIAGE AND FAMILY

In 1947 Diana saw a painting by Bernard Dunstan at the Royal Academy Summer Exhibition and sent a postcard to Bristol where he was teaching. They began to see each other in London, and in February 1949 were married, Bernard giving up his job at the art school in Bristol to join

Study of an Apple Branch
Sketch-book drawing, 1967

her. Neither his parents nor hers expressed any doubts that they could earn their living, and indeed he quickly found part-time teaching in various art schools. The wedding in Hampstead Registry Office was followed by lunch at the Café Royal. 'Bernard's father had a voice which carried and during the lunch he referred to the cricket and music commentator, Neville Cardus, as a man "who had pulled himself up by his bootlaces". Some moments later a bottle of champagne was brought to the table with the compliments of Cardus who was sitting quite at the other end of the restaurant.' The couple started their honeymoon at The Mitre in Oxford and on the following day went to see Peter Greenham, an old friend of Bernard's, who lived and worked in a wartime Nissen hut in the grounds of Magdalen College. This was the first time Diana had met Peter Greenham RA and she was deeply impressed by his paintings and drawings. 'He had a sensitive and expressive touch; there was a hint of magic in his work, and certain of his paintings became for me points of reference.' The honeymoon was spent walking from Ross-on-Wye to Monmouth along the river in glorious early spring weather.

Bernard and Diana returned to the studio to live, hanging lengths of her fabrics to create a separation between the work area and their living quarters. In February 1950 they moved into a flat at the top of the house and their first son Andrew was born. Roy Passano decided to emigrate to Canada, and shortly afterwards in 1952 Kay and William Watson moved to Kew, and Bernard and Diana went with them to occupy a flat in their house. The partnership was thus broken up, and although Diana continued to design and print by herself, the demands of a growing family made this increasingly difficult. In 1952 David was born and four years later they moved to their own house in Kew.

In September 1958 Diana took her youngest son, Robert, to nursery school and on her return found that Bernard had set up her design table in his studio. She began to work again, but sharing space proved impossible and she soon moved to a shed in the garden, and before long was selling designs to John Lines, Coles, Shand Kydd and other leading manufacturers. She was also involved on the council of the textile section of the Society of Industrial Artists. Bernard was now teaching at various art schools and Diana was teaching drawing at the Byam Shaw School of Art. She took students to draw at such places as the Courtauld Institute Galleries, the National Gallery, rehearsals at the Royal College of Music, and Bankside Power Station.

Diana acknowledges the importance of her background in textile design, and the way it has made her consider aspects of painting in a very conscious way. 'In textiles it is essential to take leading rhythms outwards from the motif. In painting the opposite is true. Some rhythms need to turn back into the rectangle, to hold the eye within the world one is making inside the picture frame. Whereas textile design should be flat, not implying real space, there is something irresistible in creating an equivalent of distance in a painting or drawing, whether by the use of planes or any other device.' The difference between painting and textile design, however, goes deeper. 'In designing textiles or wallpapers, I hoped to create a background of distinction, an atmosphere, but in painting I want to create a self-sufficient world within the rectangle, in no way just a background. I hope my spectator will be drawn into this world not only with pleasure, but with increased awareness.'

At the end of the summer term, 1965, the Principal, Maurice de Sausmarez, announced half way through the final staff meeting 'Next term I want Diana to take on the teaching of painting from drawings.' She had until the following September to prepare. That summer Bernard and Diana, she equipped with a paint box which he had made for her, set off for Arezzo for two weeks during which both would paint. For Diana it was the beginning of a new career.

Fondamenta Foscarini, Venice
Sketch-book drawing for an oil painting, 1992

Light after the Storm, Piazza San Marco, Venice
Pastel, 9 × 7½in (22.9 × 19.1cm), 1990

Diana was returning to her hotel at around 5pm after a day's drawing. As she crossed the Piazza the sun came out following a spring storm, and her eye was caught by the interesting shapes the sun and shade created on the Campanile and the Doge's Palace. The façade of the Doge's Palace and the corner of San Marco are highlighted in white, set against a cerulean blue sky, while the Campanile and flagpoles are boldly picked out in yellow, and are reflected in the wet pavement beneath. The warmth of the sunlit areas is balanced by the use of the bare paper in the shaded areas and the predominantly black and brown figures, offset by a splash of red in the child's raincoat. An evocative and luminous pastel.

Spring Flowers with Camellia
Oil, 14½ × 12¾in (36.9 × 32.4cm), 1988

Camellias are one of Diana's favourite flowers and she grows them in her garden at Kew. She finds every camellia different, even on the same bush. For this painting she chose a 'bloom of distinction', one with elegant curves, supported in this role by the daffodil, forsythia and irises behind. It was painted on her kitchen table in front of the French windows which look onto the garden. Diana enjoys painting flowers in the kitchen, as she can play the artificial light off against the natural daylight entering from the window. This balance only lasts a short time; when the daylight is at its strongest it overpowers the artificial light, but as it fades, so the electric light begins to dominate, the shadows become more purple, and the window darkens. Diana finds this balancing act both challenging and satisfying.

Notice the loose handling of the paint, the creamy, translucent texture achieved in the blooms contrasted to the deliberately less explicit handling of the table and the garden behind. Diana leads our eyes to certain focal points within the composition, and while some of the stalks and leaves take our eyes away from the blooms, the curve of the table and the shape of the shadows quickly return our gaze to the focal points. Many great artists in the past, in particular Monet, Sargent and Whistler, deliberately attempted to give the impression that their work had been achieved without struggle. Diana's flower paintings look as if they have been painted quickly and easily, belying the real control and effort which are required to give this very sense of freedom.

2
TRAVELS

With three young boys to keep occupied while on holiday, Diana Armfield's first painting trips abroad were a compromise between her painting and drawing and the demands of a family. They would take the Bedford van loaded with luggage and a tent, and explore parts of northern France, camping by rivers where the boys could spend hours in their rubber boat while Diana and Bernard worked. St Marceau, on the Sarthe near Le Mans, was a favourite spot with its river and views of the village, and the summer holiday of 1967 was spent there. They also enjoyed camping by the River Yonne which runs south from Auxerre. They usually asked permission from farmers or lock-keepers before pitching their tent and this often meant a somewhat anxious time after 5pm until they knew where they would spend the night.

Camping at
Gurgy-sur-Yonne, 1967

'Farms were often passed by with such comments as "Cows in the field", "No, not attractive", "Too muddy", and "I can see midges" until 6 o'clock drew near. There was also a certain reluctance on the part of both of us to be the one to do the asking. This was absurd because I don't remember anything but friendliness and a sympathetic interest in why we wanted to put up our tent on their land; afterwards we usually had fond memories of these kind people.

'Every now and then we went to camping sites where there was the entertainment of seeing other campers, watching the French producing elaborate meals, the neat arrangements of the Dutch and Germans and noticing that the only other less-than-smart outfits were invariably occupied by our own compatriots. Of course we suffered the usual storms that sweep France in late August, all of us outside the tent holding it up, but I rather regret that those camping days are over.'

Both their elder boys, Andrew and David, were born engineers, so a camping place which was also near a scrap heap where they could find pieces for their go-karts was an advantage. Diana did make time to paint. 'I had the paint box, a camp stool and boards, and once I had tidied up, could have several hours for myself; I hoped to work every day; sometimes just drawing, other times on small panels in oils which could be developed further once back at home in the studio from supporting drawings and written notes.'

ABROAD WITH BERNARD

As the boys got older, they were able to leave them in London with friends and go on short painting trips by themselves. In 1968 they went to Pienza and Montichiello in golden autumn weather.

'It was an absolute revelation; the undulating bare ploughed slopes, the lovely hill towns and villages, the golden stubble, all set against a blue early autumn sky. I have relished that light ever since. On that trip I was able to paint all day long. In 1969 we went to Volterra where the landscape was more patterned, more akin to textile design. I was exploring the language of oil painting, but for some time I still looked mainly for pattern and flat design in the subject. Even now I would like to combine the two ways of looking; flat areas on which to play the brush marks. I often start a painting intending to keep it simple, but before long find I am breaking up the flat areas with modifying brush strokes. My earlier work was more patterned, but also, I think, rather clumsy. In refining the shapes, I have lost something of the simplicity. Perhaps I need to return to more pattern.'

Diana and her husband usually spend between two and six weeks abroad on a painting trip.

'I find that six weeks is really too long; I am filling sketchbooks and making "starts" and find that I forget the urge of the first "starts" made earlier in the trip. Too much information can give me visual indigestion. If we are actually living somewhere where I can complete the works on the spot, a long trip is fine. We spend a month in the Rockies, when we visit our son Bob and his family and are in one place where I can finish paintings as well as gather information. For me the perfect length of an exploring painting trip is about three weeks.'

St Marceau
Oil sketch, 8 ×10in
(20.3 × 25.4cm), 1967

The choice of hotel is important (see *Hôtel des Antiques*, page 34). Diana is much affected by architecture and her spirits fall if the only available accommodation is a modern hotel with uninteresting interiors and views. They look for hotels with charm, often a small family-run affair in an old part of the town. Bernard works on hotel bedroom pictures, so the style of furniture, the furnishings, the views from the windows and the way the light enters the room are all considerations. They have certain favourites such as the Cisterna in the main square of San Gimignano. They both like to be in a town centre rather than outside so that they can enjoy the evening *passagiata* and can draw in the cafés and restaurants. They discovered the Hôtel Moderne et Pigeon in Limoux near Carcassone, a clean hotel with a certain old-fashioned grandeur. The staircase is decorated with murals; the bedrooms are large with big French windows hung with net curtains, overlooking a courtyard where people eat, so Diana can draw them from

◁ *Hôtel des Antiques, St Rémy de Provence*
Oil, 13¾ × 11¾in (34.9 × 29.8cm) 1992–93

When Bernard and Diana stayed in this grand old rambling hotel, they were put into a pavilion where they took their breakfast overlooking the main building. This fresh and lively oil captures the faded elegance of the building, bathed in strong Provençal sunshine, the light gravel path reflecting the morning heat and the guests heading towards the swimming pool. The painting was started on the spot, Diana establishing the main colours and tonal values, but was finished in the studio where the figures were added.

This oil clearly reveals the beauty of Diana's brush strokes, which appear at the same time quite free, but which also define and suggest. Notice also her use of the toned board beneath which is allowed to show through, and the play between the bright, warm sunlit areas and the purples and violets of the shaded areas.

▷ *The Road to the Village, France*
Oil, 10 × 10½in (25.4 × 26.7cm), 1989

A delightful composition suggesting the heat and peace of rural France when life comes to a halt during the midday sun. Diana enjoys the contrast between the pale colours of the road and tree trunks and the rich greens of leaves and grass. Notice the broad brush strokes which suggest rather than define and which keep the paint surface of the picture alive. The houses of the village are broadly rendered in single marks with the brush, while the foreground is a subtle play between the sunlit road and shadows of purples and pinks.

the bedroom window. Also near Carcassone at St Félix-Lauragais there is the Auberge du Poids Public which has charming old-fashioned rooms overlooking orchards and fields on the outskirts of the village. Finding reasonable accommodation in Venice is more difficult. For several years Diana and Bernard stayed at the Metropole or

Diana Armfield and
Bernard Dunstan outside
Pisa, 1968

Londra Palace taking rooms which overlooked the Riva degli Schiavoni and the Lagoon. Today, however, the prices are so high for rooms with lagoon views that this is no longer possible and so they explore cheaper accommodation.

Like most artists, Diana Armfield has certain areas and countries where she feels most at home, and both France, with its early associations, and Italy play an important part in her work. One of the regions of France she most enjoys is the area around Carcassone where she can paint the rolling hills, usually with a little village and church spire to provide an architectural element, vineyards and glimpses of the distant mountains. She has in fact painted all over the South of France (see, for instance, *The Road to the Village*, page 35), around Collioure, into Provence, and further west around Albi and the Lot et Garonne. Italy is another favourite painting ground, around San Gimignano, Siena and further south round Orvieto, standing on its great rock (see *Distant View of Orvieto*, page 123). They have also found Spain rewarding: Ronda in the south where the town with its church rising out of the fields of corn and sunflowers captivated her, although she is not attracted by the very white Moorish–looking Spanish houses. In 1993 they explored in northern Spain (see *Picnic Place in Northern Spain*, page 39). She enjoyed the contrast between the cultivated landscape and the areas of dramatic wilderness, but they both felt the beautiful medieval villages lacked the animation of their Italian or French equivalents, and seemed over-dominated by the otherwise excellent Parador hotels.

FINDING THE SUBJECT

Once they have found a hotel, Bernard and Diana establish a flexible working pattern. In the morning they have breakfast in their room and Bernard will make drawings of the room with Diana getting up. After strolling about in the town buying the picnic and perhaps drawing, they set off in the car to find a place for the day to settle down to work. Diana is the driver and she is constantly on the look-out for the ideal place. 'It is like hunting; you sense that at the end of a lane there will be something for you. I stop the car and walk about looking for possibilities. Colour and light are vital, and if there is marvellous colour I hardly need a subject. The picnic is important as it helps me to feel that the place is ours, also giving me time to absorb the subject before starting to paint.'

Diana is fascinated by vineyards, especially the play of the sprays of vines against architecture in the distance (see *Orvieto through Tall Vines*, page 38). 'I like the way light and shadows create big patterns which contrast with the small flickering forms of the vine leaves in sunshine; the pale soil between the rows of vines helps to make a needed contrast. Vines are the devil to paint, but infinitely beguiling.' She also works amongst the olive trees; they are equally challenging. 'Olive trees catch the light quite differently every minute; look up and assess, mix a colour, have a final look and find that they've changed completely from silver blue-grey to a golden green.' Architecture plays a role in these landscapes: she refers to buildings that grow out of the ground and to stone or brick warmed by the sun, and says that they provide a man-made foil to nature's rhythms and patterns.

Diana also looks for vistas in the landscapes and it is noticeable that often she makes the focal point in the distance or middle distance rather than in the foreground. She thinks this might be because she is long-sighted.

'In the hot summer of 1976 we were working in Siena and the area nearby called Le Crete. It was over 90 degrees in the town and we were pleased to get into the country. Le Crete is an extraordinary landscape with clay hills creating strange shapes. I was looking forward to painting there, but when we arrived, the distant views were completely lost in a heat haze, and I found it very difficult to work. Bernard asked why I couldn't concentrate on the foreground, but my eyes are invariably drawn into the distance.'

With the picnic over Diana starts work, usually beginning on a panel which will be the main painting of the day, although it may be carried on with later in the studio. Getting the composition of a landscape. established is important and Diana may use her hands to frame the subject. When she was teaching she noticed that students tend to choose wide views; she encouraged them to close in and select much less of their original subject. 'Come down until just before you begin to lose meaning; the wider the view, the more alike the forms become in shape and size. The smaller the view, the greater the variety of

shapes within it and the more significant each becomes.' In the late afternoon as the sun begins to sink and the landscape turns golden, Diana will often make quick oil sketches to capture the colours before they go. There is sometimes a conflict of interests at this time of the day, with Bernard keen to return to see the town at dusk or to get back to the hotel, and Diana anxious to capture the last moments before the sunset. Once they have returned to the town they may draw the animated scene of the evening *passagiata*, put down something of the effects of dusk and draw in a restaurant over their evening meal.

CITIES

Some cities appeal to Diana, especially those with parks, street cafés and an outdoor way of life. Paris is one of her favourite places; she likes to draw in the Luxembourg

Semur, France
Drawing for a painting, 1968

◁ *Orvieto through Tall Vines*
Oil, 16 × 14in (40.6 × 35.6cm), 1989

In many ways this is a 'classic' Armfield landscape with all the elements the artist enjoys – a melting blue distance with some architectural elements, a profusion of tall vines spilling their leaves in abundance over the man-made order of the vine-yard, and warm sunlit earth which is played off against the shadows. The artist has commented on the problems of painting vines (page 37) and here we see how she masses the areas of sunlit and shaded leaves to create a strong composition. Notice the richness of the foreground. The warm ochre earth is played off against blues, greens, pinks and browns and all the while the breadth of the brushwork creates a freshness and vitality which makes the viewer wish he was standing on that very spot.

▷ *Picnic Place below San Gimignano*
Oil, 23¾ × 20¾in (60.3 × 52.7cm), 1993

'This site we made into our outdoor studio and picnic place while staying in San Gimignano; the high hedge offered shade for the best part of the day. I set my easel up and by just moving a few yards or looking a little to the left or right, there seemed to be an infinite number of possibilities, all of them redolent of the landscape there. I think in all I must have done at least eight paintings from there. This was the most ambitious, but done from drawings a year later, with one or two of the smaller sketches round about to remind me of the special colour.'

△ *Picnic Place in Northern Spain*
Oil, 11½ × 9½in (29.2 × 24.2cm), 1993

'The first picnic place which also suggests a painting
sets the tone for that particular trip, and one ceases
to be just a traveller passing through. It was early
May and yet still spring time with flowering
chestnuts and fresh pale greens in the landscape. I
had my vista to the distant village and enjoyed the
contrast between the darker thick foliage of the
chestnut tree giving us shade and the line of golden
planes opposite. This painting was started on the
spot but finished from a sketch-book note.' (See
page 36.)

PAINTING IN VENICE

Venice is a recurring, consistent subject and she visits the city most years during the winter or early spring when there are fewer tourists. She is very conscious of the way the light reflects off the water into the shadowed areas giving luminosity, and she finds it rewarding to work in the muted sunshine, the fogs and mists of the winter months with their particular magic and mystery. She says the brilliant summer sunshine can be marvellous but it can also break up the forms and make composing difficult. Like others, she enjoys a busy city dominated by people rather than cars, and it is a relief to be able to see the 'feet' of the architecture and the way the buildings 'sit'. Diana is not concerned about the number of painters who have worked in Venice before her.

'I feel that I can make it my own, but I do avoid the companionship of dear painter friends in Venice, as I think their vision, which I normally enjoy, might then impinge on my own [see *Cat on the Giudecca*, page 79 and *Umbrellas Up*, page 82]. It is enough to feel the influence of the three great interpreters of Venice: Turner, Whistler and Sickert.

'I admire the way Sickert puts down quite large flat areas, on which he virtually "handwrites" in the smaller architectural forms, suggesting doors, windows and other details. I have at times tried to emulate this approach, which may sound simple, but in fact needs the master's selective eye and sure touch. I try to "write" into wet paint rather than dry, as I find that for me it "marries" more convincingly with the paint underneath. Sickert's marks are beautiful as well as revealing subject matter and I am always intrigued by his most individual and odd colour relationships which bring magic to the low key of his paintings. Apart from the interiors which vary, I often see Venice in a high, light-hearted key.' (See *Canal near the Zattere*, page 43, and *Campo San Giacomo dell'Orio*, page 87.)

Montechiello
Oil on board, 6 × 7in
(15.2 × 17.8cm), 1968

Gardens and in the Tuileries, watching children playing after school or out with their grandparents. She talks of sunlight on the blond gravel and the deep shadows cast by the chestnut trees. Both Bernard and Diana enjoy short trips abroad to explore European cities, taking with them just sketch-books. 'Amsterdam provided the Rijksmuseum with its marvellous Rembrandts and a rich Art Deco café, Madrid charming squares and parks, shellfish meals and Goya in the Prado.' In 1985 they went further afield as Artists in Residence to Perth in Western Australia. Diana came away having done a lot of work and with a real affection for the place. Her memories were of wine-dark seas (see *The Ocean*, page 78) and attractive athletic people, young and old alike enjoying open-air life by the water.

Venice is full of subjects for Diana and she still works in the Piazza as well as in the smaller campi across the Grand Canal, or in the side canals off the Zattere. One of the problems of painting in Venice is that crowds quickly form to see what is going on, but Diana, who likes to keep her eye on the subject while painting, tries not to reply to the questions and comments. 'Having a crowd looking at me painting changes the way I work; I begin to paint with a certain bravura which becomes quite a strain. I remember once painting while noticing a crowd out of the corner of my eye; soon most disappeared except for one who stayed on. When I finally finished, I looked round and saw that "the person" was just a bollard!'

John Ward RA has described the Piazza San Marco as 'the architectural nude, obvious but never the same', and quite a few of Diana's paintings and pastels are based in the Piazza.

'If I am taking in the whole of San Marco I look for big effects of light and shadow to cross the small shapes of the architecture. This helps turn the complicated scene into something broader, simpler and more manageable. Usually I take in only narrow vistas or corners, sometimes as backgrounds to the animated scenes on the paving or, more often, I'm caught by some special effect of light, perhaps after a storm, which reveals something I haven't seen before [see *Light after the Storm*, page 30]. From the Piazzetta, the winter sun setting, almost behind the Salute, is entrancing and most years I find myself having yet one more go at it.' (See *Winter Sunset*, page 43.)

During the day Diana and Bernard will go their own ways and work separately, arranging to meet, weather permitting, for a picnic lunch on the Zattere or down the Riva. One of the most inviting periods for Diana is dusk. 'It is a miraculous time as the lights begin to come on, but I only have about ten minutes before the artificial light takes over completely from daylight. We usually arrange to

meet in the Piazza towards dusk.' (See *Winter Sunset*, page 43.) There are two famous cafés there which both feature in Diana's work – Quadri's and Florian's.

'Florian's is dark, opulent and richly decorated. I sit inside, order one cup of tea with lemon and regularly ask for more hot water, intending to spend several hours there drawing the people and the interior [see *Conversation at Florian's*, page 22]. The waiters are usually very accommodating and let me stay, even allowing me to change my place when a different table becomes vacant. Quadri's has

Near Alegria, Picnic Place
Sketch-book drawing, 1993, for *Picnic Place in Northern Spain* (page 39).

San Giorgio Maggiore from the Riva, Venice
Oil, 6 × 8in (15.2 × 20.3cm), 1993

This is a much-painted view, but the artist has managed to say something new and different.

Instead of concentrating upon the architectural details of this well-known vista, Diana has shared with us her sense of elation at seeing the brilliant blues and greens of the lagoon set against the purple-blues of the buildings seen against the

morning sun. The freshness of this small panel is enhanced by the spontaneous brushwork which allows the warm burnt sienna ground of the panel to show through, and by so doing, adds intensity to the colours in the water.

△ *Canal near the Zattere, Venice*
Oil, 9½ × 8in (24.2 × 20.3cm), 1993

'This is a view that I have looked at many times over the years, admired, but not seen how to compose, so left alone. Suddenly something about the strong glowing sunlight on the left wall, carried on over the bridge to the shadowed side, made it both possible and irresistible to do something with.'

▷ *Winter Sunset, Venice*
Oil, 9¼ × 7in (23.5 × 17.8cm), 1993

On page 41 Diana describes her special affection for this particular winter view of Venice.

Near San Polo, Venice
Sketch-book drawing for
a pastel, 1992

a different atmosphere; it used to be the Austrian café and still retains a certain Austrian charm. The people there are often dressed with more care, lovers or honeymoon couples, with fewer anoraks and rucksacks. The clientele make it more of an occasion, so it also becomes so for me. One of the delights of working from drawings later in the studio is that I can relive those moments. I might also invent incidents or build up possible relationships between the people who inhabit my pastels. This interest in people is perhaps new in my work; I wasn't doing this ten years ago.'

Having lived in London for many decades, it cannot be considered as 'travel', but Diana's pastels of Fortnum and Mason's restaurant in Piccadilly should be mentioned (see *Ladies at Lunch*, page 94, and *Lunch at Fortnum's*, page 115). For many years Diana used the restaurant as a West End base, relaxing on the pink sofas and having lunch there on Private View Days of the Royal Academy. She has always been taken by its old-fashioned furnishings, which include paintings of elephants by David Shepherd, ship pictures, pink sofas and waitresses in black and white.

'I have been doing drawings in Fortnum's for many years, and several times there has been a lady with a smart white beret who was aware I was drawing her and enjoyed posing. John Brandler, the art dealer, usually has a table there for his guests on the first Private View Day of the Academy; one year I did a pastel drawing of him with his guests. The Irish manageress of the restaurant takes an interest in our work and always asks whether we've sold anything yet. Just as in Florian's or Quadri's in Venice, I enjoy speculating on the relationship between people there. One day there were two ladies in hats in full gossip; also there was a daughter or niece who was obviously out of the conversation and very bored. I did a pastel of the group which I called *The Confidential Conversation*.' (See page 102.)

TRIPS TO THE UNITED STATES

For some years Diana and Bernard have been making trips to the United States to visit their son and his family who live in Jackson Hole in the Rockies (see *Aspens along the Path in the Rockies*, page 122). Diana finds America very stimulating and the people open and friendly; she is also amazed by the charm of many of the towns.

'Georgetown in Washington is more English than many towns in England; I noticed the weatherboard houses with their charming fantasies, shrubs and creepers. I also enjoyed San Francisco with its extraordinary light and colour; the constant smog results in a band of strange violet greys in the sky above the horizon. Bob went to the States, where his wife comes from, to make musical instruments; he then turned to furniture and has always been a true craftsman. He lives with his family in Jackson Hole, under the Grand Tetons, and we are lent, by his wife's parents, their summer log cabin. There are vast views there which I find difficult to manage, but I can limit the scale by painting the views through the aspen trees. These are as teasing and beguiling as olives; the trunks changing colour from moment to moment. The colours all round are beautiful in the intense mountain light and the tones stronger than anything I've experienced in Europe.'

In 1989 Diana and Bernard were Artists in Residence at Riverside Meadows, Jackson Hole, and Diana was able to paint views along the river lined by the feathery cottonwood trees which she calls 'Turneresque'. She also draws in the museums and art galleries in Chicago and New York. 'Americans have a different body language from Europeans and I see this as soon as I bring the drawings home and compare them with my sketch-book notes of gallery goers in Europe.' (See *The Art Institute of Chicago*, page 103.)

Diana has also drawn in the Plaza Hotel, New York (see *Deciding on the Menu*, page 95) which has a rather grand tea-room not unlike Fortnum's. 'I enjoy its old-fashioned opulence; there is usually a pianist or a trio playing, and China tea served in porcelain.' The journey to and from the United States also provides interesting material as they sometimes travel on the QE2 rather than flying. She finds the clientele full of interest to watch and is able to draw in the various restaurants, tea-rooms and on deck, but adds 'Here I do have to respond to onlookers; it would not do to be off-hand to staff or other passengers.' (See *The Deck Café on the QE2*, page 90, and *Buffet Lunch on the QE2*, page 91.)

Below Montalcino
Sketch-book drawing, 1991

◁ *Mark on the Path, Jackson Hole*
Oil, 8¾ × 8¾in (22.2 × 22.2cm), 1989

'This is the small version done on the spot from which a much larger painting was developed. We have visited our family in the Rockies a number of times, and this path, cut through the grass to make a way for us, leading from our log cabin to the larger log house, has become quite significant. The aspens are relatively short-lived, so there are considerable changes from one visit to the next, but each time the trees have a way of composing themselves into interesting and varied intervals to be noticed and made something of. The fencing is characteristic of the region and makes a useful foil to the aspens. One or other grandson is often on the path.'

▷ *Norah's Fish Inn, Jackson Hole*
Pastel, 8 × 9½in (20.3 × 24.2cm), 1991

'A typical Western eatery where both the local residents and the dude ranchers meet their friends for hot spiced soup and toasted sandwiches. It was our daughter-in-law's pale violet shirt that set off the scene and I placed our Bob among the other diners. The splendid Tiffany-style lampshades were what first caught my attention against the dark wood of the interior, but as sometimes happens, they had to be reduced in importance in the working out of the pastel and left for a future attempt.'

3

WALES

Cottage at Llwynhir,
North Wales

Some years before World War II, Harold Armfield, seeing the potential for water power from the many streams in North Wales, provided installations for some of the larger farms and became known as 'Mr Armfield, electric man'. Combining holiday with work, Diana's mother accompanied him and they came to love the country, its people and language. 'My mother claimed a measure of Welsh descent, and by an odd coincidence the Williams who kept the sub-post office in the village of Parc said we were related on my father's side.'

The Armfields walked the mountains and fields, and following pre-war custom called at farms for tea and conversation. On one occasion they were told that the community of Parc regarded the tumble-down cottage, Llwynhir, as an eyesore and disgrace; no one locally was able or willing to save it from collapse. It fell to the Armfields to restore it over the next year or so. Taking on another similar derelict property across the river, they handed Llwynhir over to Diana in 1943 and in due course moved permanently to their own house Ty Newydd, across the river from Llwynhir, near the village of Parc above Lake Bala, where they lived for some thirty years. Both houses lie within the boundary of Snowdonia National Park.

Diana and her family have been associated with Parc for over fifty years and her cottage in Wales is an important part of her life.

'I was brought up in the country, and although I enjoy London, I need a country base. When I first used to go there, apart from the local community, I knew only my parents and their friends. Now I have a wider circle, and my sister Kay and her husband are neighbours up the Arenig mountain. Each year we spend some weeks there at Christmas, and after the spring in Kew has turned to summer, we go again to catch the late spring in Wales. These two seasons are times when the colour is at its most special to Wales but even in the height of summer, when we are there for longer, the trees, even the sycamores, remain fresh. In between the times together, I go for a week at a time, ostensibly to have uninterrupted painting. Perhaps the days do seem longer during those weeks. I am able to engross myself for hour after hour in the studio or stay out beyond a reasonable hour in the evenings, but I should probably feel lonely if there weren't the frequent knocks on the door from neighbours and the children in the village.'

She has become noted as a painter of Wales and is a member of the Royal Cambrian Academy. One of their closest friends, Kyffin Williams RA, lives in Anglesey. 'He is well known and much appreciated throughout North Wales, not merely in the art world, so that when he visits us his arrival is always noted and remarked upon.' He is President of the Royal Cambrian Academy and has done much to improve its fortunes by organizing the move into their newly built gallery in Conwy. Some years ago Diana was honoured by being given a retrospective exhibition held jointly with Bernard Dunstan in Newtown and Welshpool. She has also exhibited at the Tegfryn Gallery, Menai Bridge, and at the Albany Gallery in Cardiff.

In 1990–91 Diana was invited to represent the Contemporary Art Society of Wales, acquiring paintings by contemporary artists on a limited budget. The choice of work was entirely free but had to be 'justified' at a 'Presentation' the following year.

'I hoped to choose from artists who had yet to be represented, could claim some Welsh connection, and whose work reflected an admiration for some aspect of life. It proved a rewarding but somewhat nerve-racking experience; buying is quite as fraught as selling. However it led me to visit the studio of Anthony Eyton RA who can claim descent from the Welsh kings. His studio begins just inside the front door of a large house in Brixton and extends down the corridors and up the stairs into all the rooms. I chose a luminous watercolour beach scene with figures. I also visited David Shutt in his small house on the other side of Arenig mountain. I was familiar with the

Llwynhir Trees, Spring
Pencil drawing, 1973

Sheep in the Snow
Oil, 11¾ × 9½in (29.8 × 24.2cm), 1986

Diana always hopes to paint some snow pictures when she is at her cottage in Wales at Christmas and again in February. This oil was painted looking out of a window there. In summer the sheep appear very white against the vivid green grass, but in winter they become darker and more golden when seen against the snow.

The palette is restricted to white, earth colours and some subtle touches of blues, and the composition centres on the blackbird perched on a post. The brushwork is kept free and controlled and Diana suggests rather than defines, leaving much to our imagination. The picture is suffused in that sense of stillness and quiet which comes after a heavy fall of snow.

△ *Sheep up the Bank, North Wales*
Pastel, 7 × 7in (17.8 × 17.8cm), 1992

'The sheep usually make off when I try to get near enough to draw them, but this time they got themselves jammed against the hedge, and so stood looking at me, fixed for long enough for me to make some sort of useful note.

'Afterwards I drew the hedge at leisure directly on to Canson paper. It was the intense light of the spring day against the simple area of blue-grey shadow which had caught my attention as well as the sheep.'

△ *Sheep in the Gully above Llanycil*
Oil, 17½ × 19½in (44.5 × 49.6cm), 1991

Diana is attracted to the vivid colours of the Welsh landscape which are a result of the abundant rainfall which keeps the foliage verdant. In this landscape the artist contrasts the rich green of the grass and trees with the dramatic white of the sheep, rocks and fence posts. Our eyes are led gently up the gully into the distance, but are brought back by the tree on the left. Notice the way in which depth is created by the use of transparent layers of paint in the foreground; the warm ochre ground is overlaid with touches of green and blue-green over which the more opaque whites and greys are floated.

cramped conditions. Perhaps practical difficulties induce a greater obsession. I realised that the only artist I knew well with a purpose-built studio was Ken Howard RA who certainly makes use of it. Most of us manage in ordinary rooms, not even insisting on the "essential" north light.'

Part of the enjoyment of working in Wales is the contact with the people, whom Diana finds so hospitable, helpful and full of fun. 'They are always smiling and joking or pulling my leg. The Welsh people make my life there pleasurable; they are part of the romance I have with the country.' She enjoys the Welsh interest in music, and her only regret is that, because of her inability to learn the language, she is not able to take any part in drama and music in Parc where there is a thriving tradition of performing and competing in the Eisteddfod.

PAINTING THE WELSH LANDSCAPE

The cottage is a 'two up, two down' stone building to which they have added an additional stone L-shaped room with windows on three sides. This has become her studio. Diana works there, often bringing unfinished panels from London as well as working on Welsh landscapes. It is larger than her Kew studio and with its natural daylight she finds that she sees works in progress, brought from London, in a different light. She often paints in the fields around Bala. 'I always ask permission from the farmers before I start painting. Invariably they will come to look at what I'm doing, standing a few feet from my easel, looking at the view and philosophizing or poeticizing about it. I find most Welsh people are highly articulate, more articulate than visual, or rather, they quickly turn the visual into words.' She sometimes sets up her easel on the slopes of Arenig, painting the tumbling rocks, which catch the light, and sheep seen against the vivid green grass. Spring she finds particularly exhilarating in Wales; the golden tones of the trees and the peppermint green of the

Sheep in the Argoed Field
CarbOthello pencil on Canson paper, 1993

parlour as the Puws, who had years before alerted my parents to Llwynhir, had retired there from their farm, remaining there until a few years ago. It was strange to see the Puws' table in such a different setting, and to be taken upstairs to what had been a bedroom and was now a tiny studio. I chose, but was only just allowed to buy, an intense measured drawing of rocks in the stream. I was reminded of Euan Uglow and Patrick Symons RA in his reluctance to part with a drawing. "I can't commit myself to finishing with it before your 'Presentation' next year; I may not have resolved the painting for several years." One other studio I visited was that of Maurice Sheppard, which was also a former bedroom. I chose a "six-footer" of gypsies in the woods at Haverford West, and did wonder afterwards how Maurice could have produced it in such grass set against a high-toned sky, washed by rain and unsullied by pollution (see *Sheep in the Gully*, page 51).

Diana paints the landscape with its rocks, sheep and trees rather than the cottages and villages of Wales. She was once commissioned to paint the house of George Holt of the Liverpool shipping family, benefactors of the Walker Art Gallery: he remained a trustee until he died.

'He was an interesting man who, like my mother, studied the Welsh language; they read Welsh literature together. He was very conscious of the environment and bought land in the district to preserve it from development, while allowing the previous owners to carry on farming it. When teased with being "an old Tory" he countered by saying that in his youth he had been responsible for fitting out a ship for the government side during the Spanish Civil War. His life was something of a contrast to our own, regularly shooting and fishing. He suffered delicate health yet as a sportsman was to be seen, a tall thin man with two dogs at his heels, striding the rough mountain slopes. His housekeeper cooked the most splendid Sunday lunches for his frequent guests, among them curators of museums. We revelled in his open-handed invitations and made many friends at his table. He surrounded himself with choice works of art of all kinds including furniture, china, sculpture and pictures. In the corner of his dining-room hung a little watercolour by Turner, which for me illuminated the whole room. Occasionally I accompanied him on a walk, for him to collect fungi for supper and firewood and for me to notice "possibilities" for paintings.

'He commissioned me to paint his house and he took it very well that my painting was as much of his trees as his house. He hung it in the dining-room so that I saw it each time I lunched there. At the opposite end from the Turner watercolour hung a portrait by Ruskin Spear of Barbara Castle MP with her flaming red hair, a splendid, almost Expressionist work which he was proud to have bought on

the last day of the Royal Academy Summer Exhibition. Another commission came from the Price family at Rhiwlas who asked me to paint the landscape near their house, having seen some of my Welsh paintings at Browse and Darby in London. It was a rewarding experience as it took me to parts I hadn't explored before.

'One of the problems of painting the landscape in Wales is the weather. On a rainy day, I will often work on a painting of flowers, and the next day the weather might change, and I will be keen to work outside, but have to continue with the flowers. When we first went to Wales, the hedges and verges were full of wild flowers, and the

Outside the new room, Llwynhir, 1970

△ *Snow at Christmas, Llwynhir*
Oil, 11 × 11½in (27.9 × 29.2cm), 1993–94

'The gift of snow at Christmas is not to be missed. The unexpected luminous colour of the sycamore trunk, hardly darker than the snow, caught my admiration; the blue of the distant Berwyn Mountains sang out behind the snow. On this occasion the view out of the bedroom window composed itself. It doesn't always! The bird did actually perch there for a moment.'

△ *Sheep Dog Working on Arenig*
Oil, 14¾ × 18¾in (37.5 × 47.6cm), 1992

'I have painted the tumbling rocks on the far side of Arenig many times and at different seasons. It is an eight mile drive and I usually choose to go in the late afternoon when the sun bathes the rocks, sheep and grass in golden light. I take my easel and do as much as I can standing up to paint on the spot. The light on that grand landscape never fails to give me a thrill of pleasure.'

Winter Sunset, Llwynhir, over Moel Menin
Oil, 5½ × 6½in (14 × 16.5cm), 1987

A delightful small oil sketch done on the spot
looking out of the cottage window. It follows in the
tradition of Constable's oil studies of the skies over
Hampstead Heath. Diana describes the problems of
painting sunsets on page 56.

generation of children who are now grown up could identify them with their Welsh names. Insecticides and ruthless hedge cutting have taken their toll. I try to contribute towards the reviving interest in the environment by offering prizes at Parc primary school for the best botanical drawings, but the verges are not yet back to the abundance of species of fifty years ago.'

PAINTING BY THE SEA

On a fine, windless day Bernard and Diana will spend a day painting on Harlech beach with its dramatic backcloth of the Snowdon range seen over the dunes. After giving Bernard a sitting in a secluded dip of a dune, Diana will hope to do an oil sketch of the marram grass on the dunes and the sea. Another favourite spot is Friog where she paints the beautiful boulders and rounded stones of the beach against the sea and sky (see *Low Cloud over Friog Beach*, page 59). Many of her sky studies are painted in Wales; she finds the skies in Wales magnificent, the colours washed clear by the rain and the way the clouds build up into spectacular formations. After a day's painting in the studio, she might drive out to where she can get a clearer view of the sunset.

'The problem with painting the sunset is the speed with which the colour changes from minute to minute and I have to work on from the memory of what I've seen a few moments before. Sometimes I think I will help myself by laying out several possible mixtures of grey-blues and grey-violets or browns of different tones, as practised by Whistler, but I find these mixtures nearly always need modifying immediately, no two sunsets ever being the same. Painting a sunset is exhilarating; there is no time to reflect, all is direct response, but inevitably a hit and miss affair. Some panels come off [see *Winter Sunset*, page 55], others are abandoned and overlaid in due course. I try to be "at the ready" with my box and in the right place, but

sometimes when all has looked promising, the shielding clouds suddenly melt away, leaving the sun to go down in a blinding blaze.'

SNOW AND FROST

Another favourite subject in Wales is snow which Diana hopes for when she goes at Christmas, in February, and even at Easter; she also finds the landscape under frost very beautiful. When the weather is particularly cold, especially if the wind is strong, she works on views from the windows of the cottage; in winter the sunset can be seen from the bathroom window.

'I used to work outside in all weather conditions, but one winter I didn't realize just how cold and numb I was; I needed thawing out so try to be more careful now. Snow often does not give the appearance of cold; it is full of reflected colours and is rarely white. Snow at sunset in particular takes on lovely pinks and golds which contrast with the shadows. I concentrate on the variations of colour within snow, and when I paint on the spot, I find these colours change all the time. This, of course, presents the problem of how you cope with change while painting: do you follow the changes or do you stick to what you first saw? Sometimes I do one, and sometimes the other, but I try not to compromise [see *Sheep in the Snow*, page 50].

'I have done the journey from Kew to Wales and back again not less than two hundred times. When I am on my own I usually break the journey near Stone in Staffordshire with a childhood friend, Jane Waley, and her husband Ralph. The stretch from Parc to Stone is richly endowed with generous farmlands and has become so familiar that I now want the time that the break gives me to stop and make something of these views. For so long they have caught my attention as I drive past, and now by sheer familiarity, have begun to mean something to me, enough at least for a drawing or sketch.'

***Sheep Wintering
across the River at
Llwynhir***
CarbOthello pencil on
Canson paper, 1994

◁ *Wild Roses from the Hedge to Parc*
Oil, 19¾ × 8½in (50.2 × 21.6cm), 1993

'There are still a variety of wild roses, even if I have to reach up further to find those that have escaped the ruthless hedge cutting. The petals tend to drop after one day, or if accidentally touched, so once started on a painting, I keep going all day long hoping to get everything securely established in its place before nightfall with the most dominant blooms almost fully realized. But however much I may concentrate on the flowers, I do have to paint what is round them with equal attention; it is still a "to and fro" process. Such ephemeral blooms make the painting a race against time, but hugely rewarding when the work "comes off".'

▷ *Low Cloud over Friog Beach*
Oil, 5¾ × 9½in (14.6 × 24.2cm)

This marvellously fresh seascape was painted quickly, in the path of an approaching storm, at Friog Beach. Diana often likes to work at Harlech, which is sandy, but when the wind is strong the sand begins to blow about, making painting impossible. Although small, this painting has great power and energy and follows a tradition of British *plein-air* painters, like William McTaggart, who captured the force of nature on canvas. The viewer's eye is drawn to the dark rain cloud on the horizon, the intensity of which is emphasized by the lighter cloud above with just a glimpse of pink and violet.

4
FLOWERS AND GARDENS

Ivy leaves
Drawing with touches of
pastel, 1992

Painting flowers is central to Diana Armfield's art, and she finds it extraordinary that so many people do not realize its importance.

'Flowers are part of nature's working; they are perfectly constructed to fulfil a practical role in nature. Most people are beguiled by their beauty and rarely take them seriously as an art form. Possibly people take their beauty for granted and don't look sufficiently to see exactly why they are beautiful; many modern painters lean superficially on the beauty of the flowers without analysing their charm. In the past flowers have been carefully examined; the flowers in the Pompeii frescoes spring to mind, as do Dürer's watercolour studies of grasses or Vuillard's use of flowers in his interiors.'

She finds the subject extremely challenging, possibly more so than any other area of her work, but the results more than justify the struggle.

The first time that Diana realized the potential of painting flowers, as opposed to using the flowers as motifs in textile designs, was when she noticed a Christmas rose on the kitchen dresser which 'called out' to be painted. Allan Gwynne-Jones saw the painting (see *Christmas Rose on the Studio Table*, page 15) and was

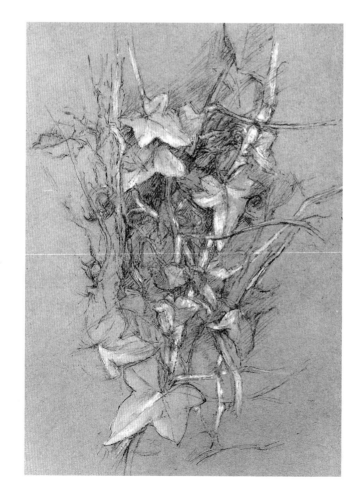

impressed, encouraging her to do further studies, and today she is one of Britain's leading painters of flowers, her work in this field always standing out at the Royal Academy Summer Exhibitions.

GATHERING AND ARRANGING THE FLOWERS

For Diana, the ideal is to walk into a room and find flowers arranged by someone else that seem just right. She admits that this happens rarely, sometimes on birthdays or at Christmas, and that usually she has to arrange them herself. She likes to pick flowers from the garden or find wild flowers and grasses, and as she is picking them she is already thinking about the arrangement. Once in a jug or glass, she will often leave them overnight in a cool place so that they 'rearrange themselves'; sometimes she is too impatient to wait and will begin to paint right away. She paints those flowers that are available in the garden or the fields, occasionally adding bought flowers.

'When I am picking flowers, I am aware that I'll probably want at least one larger bloom to which I can add subsidiary flowers; perhaps a camellia, which I grow in the garden in Kew and which flowers as early as February. If there is nothing growing in the garden to make up a bunch, I look for spring flowers in the shops. Many of these, including freesias, daffodils and jonquils, are inviting, but present-day growers too often force the colours and sizes of blooms such as gladiola, even pansies and polyanthus, and then I am not attracted by them. I also grow early flowering iris stylosa which start off a delicate violet-blue, but change as they open. This presents a challenge to paint, but is always worth a try.'

There are many flowers that Diana paints; pansies with their intense patterned 'faces', primroses, dandelions and bright celandines in the springtime. Later come the roses, and she grows several old varieties against the grey stone

walls of their place in Wales (see *Summer Roses in Wales*, page 86), and the hedgerow there provides several species of wild rose to mix with the wild flowers and grasses, the pink campion, foxgloves and daisies (see *Wild Flowers with a Welsh Rose*, page 127).

On her travels abroad she fills a jam jar with wild flowers from the roadside to put in the front of the car, and if there is a wet day takes them into the hotel room to paint. 'Making compositions from wild flowers found by the roadside is not always easy as they are often small and all roughly the same size. I find it helpful to place them in such a way that the light creates some massing of tone.' (See *Roadside Flowers*, page 70.)

COMPOSITION

With the arrangements which Diana makes for herself rather than coming across 'ready made', she will probably try them out in different places – on the kitchen table, in the studio, on a window sill and, on one occasion because the weather was too fine to be indoors, on an outside sill. She looks for 'links' between the arrangement of flowers and the setting, judging whether she can see an overall pattern, and a stability of design, which can then be broken across by the spilling over of the flowers, leaves and stalks, rather in the way that a gardener puts up a trellis for a clematis to ramp over. She feels that composing is partly an intuitive process, and has to see it before starting. Sometimes she likes to have two different light sources; daylight from a window on one side, and artificial light on the other. 'The light from the window fills half the shadow areas with cool light, and the electric light warms those on the opposite side.' (See *Christmas Flowers on the Piano*, page 19, and *April Flowers on the Sill*, page 63.) For the setting she will sometimes use a table with a window behind, looking from a fairly high viewpoint which emphasizes a steep perspective. At other times she will place the flowers in front of some books or shelves.

A Rose for Harold

Oil, 11½in × 9in (29.2 × 22.9cm), 1981

This picture was painted as Diana's father, Harold Armfield, was coming to the end of his long life. 'This was a strange time. I could only snatch the odd short hour for painting over the three or four days I needed, so with a mind already full, the two concentrations were mingled. The rose opened to a full flush and held gloriously without wilting or dropping. It was still there days later to give pleasure in a fresh bunch. I felt that something of this time of heightened awareness showed in the work, which has remained a favourite.'

△ *Pansies, Sweet-Peas and Roses in a Jar*
Oil, 13¼ × 11¾in (33.6 × 29.8cm), 1989

The intense purples and blues of the pansies are contrasted with the creamy white of the rose, while the sweet-peas and leaves spill out across the composition. The curve of the table in the upper part of the picture is reflected in the full, rounded shapes of the pansies and rose, while the base of the jar, painted parallel to the picture plane, provides an anchor in the composition.

◁ *April Flowers on the Sill, Llwynhir*
Oil, 16½ × 14in (41.9 × 35.6cm), 1991

In a similar way, 'active' areas of the composition are played off against 'passive' areas. Sometimes the background will be quite unexpected, such as the Christmas cards seen in *Flowers on the Christmas Table* (page 71) or a stack of mounting board seen in the studio, but whatever the setting, it plays an important part in the composition.

Diana has a wide collection of jugs and small cups which she picks up in junk shops, has inherited or has been given by old students and friends. She used to paint mostly smaller arrangements and has many eighteenth- and nineteenth-century English china cups; more recently she has begun to paint larger works so now looks out for large but beautiful crocks. She enjoys painting china decorated with flowers as it is necessary to make the distinction between the 'real' flowers and the painted flowers; this is an interesting problem. Association plays an important part in her work; she puts the flowers in a piece of china bought abroad or an Italian wine jug and this brings back memories of a trip. Similarly she likes to paint flowers brought by friends or associated with a particular birthday or Christmas. 'I need to have a level of association as well as visual delight to want to begin working, but once having started to paint, the flowers begin to exert their own personalities, making their own associations. Sometimes it can feel like painting a "conversation piece".'

Diana often uses two jugs, glasses or jars; a main one and a subsidiary holding perhaps just one or two small flowers (see *Kingcups and Primroses at Llwynhir*, page 67). This concept of a main theme with a secondary theme, which echoes music as well as many aspects of life, plays a part in many of her paintings of flowers, not only in the foreground objects but also in the arrangement of the blooms themselves. In some paintings she likes to have a particular bloom which dominates; however it must be supported by smaller blooms and leaves or shapes in the setting which can act as foils. She finds that the eye

Young chestnuts
Pencil drawing, 1970

'I am very conscious of the need for a strong framework which is then modified by the flowers, leaves and grasses. I begin by establishing some very definite things within the rectangle and then set about breaking into this framework. I see this all as part of the "to and fro" of painting, and it is not a different approach from composing a landscape or townscape in which the structure is broken by, or played off against, the organic elements of people, dogs or pigeons.'

tends to go directly to where the lightest and darkest parts meet and she finds herself looking for these focal points. Once the composition is seen, Diana begins to put in a very few but precise guidelines. These are the framework and may include the main stems as they cross some stable feature in the background, or the edge of an important shadow and their relationship with the base of the jug or jar. Once she has established the framework, she turns her attention to the blooms.

'I don't allow anything to become over-explicit, and enjoy the elements of "lost and found". If necessary I will add further flowers either to break up intervals or to create new rhythms. People often think that they know flowers, but I like to feel that some parts of the painting are mysterious and lost. I don't want to reveal all; I want to suggest and beguile. Certain parts of the painting must be clear, contrasted by areas of understatement. I hope my viewers will use their own imaginations.'

Her painting methods vary from picture to picture. At times she will work straight into a painting with no preliminary massing or laying in; at other times she will rub in a mixture of paint to create the mass of leaves before attempting the blooms. Some paintings are finished in one session (see *Nasturtiums*, page 26), while others might be worked on, and changed, over a number of days, weeks, even months (see *Camellias in a Winter Bunch on the Studio Table*, page 6, *A Rose for Harold*, page 62, and *Flowers in September from round the Log Cabin*, page 66). While many might think that painting flowers is a relaxing pursuit, there are many pressures involved. Often there is the pressure of time, the need to finish before the flowers die; at other times she finds that the composition or tonality is not working and that the picture has to be put aside and rethought from memory at a later date. She feels that painting flowers is more stressful than painting landscapes but, despite this, infinitely rewarding.

Rosa Gallica
Oil, 12¼ × 9¼in
(31.1 × 23.5cm), 1973

These roses are from
Kyffin Williams' garden.

RHYTHM AND MOVEMENT

Diana brings about a sense of movement in her paintings by stressing leading lines, by use of recession, by carefully noticing and controlling the intervals and occasionally by tilting the perspective.

'An artist has to be aware of what is happening with the intervals; human beings have a tendency to create regular intervals, possibly as part of a desire to establish stability, but when we see them in a painting we are disappointed because such monotony does not correspond to life. An artist has to emphasize movement in a painting because,

Flowers in September from round the Log Cabin

Oil, 15¾ × 12½in (39.9 × 31.8cm), 1993

'This painting went through many stages, being further built up in the Kew studio after our return from the United States. The interior of the log cabin is inevitably rather dark; a strong light strikes in for a few feet from a south-east window making it seem even darker inside; it is quite difficult to see the palette while working. The little yellow pansies grow in Kaidi's garden and I wanted to make something of all the different golds and yellows against the cool dark purple pansies and the bluish shadow areas. I had the urge to paint on a larger scale than sometimes, so Kaidi, our daughter-in-law and also a painter, gave me one of her prepared toned panels. It felt very different from my own or Bernard's so I found myself painting with a different touch until I had some paint going; this proved invigorating. I rather enjoyed the "tooth" of the surface. The correspondence between the curling dried leaf running through to a bright white flower and the glass handle of the jug caught my attention immediately; I held onto this whatever else I altered. The tube of red paint in the foreground is intended to link with the pink perennial sweet-pea and draw the eye down. There is a little play going on between the green leaves of the pansies on the left and the light edge of an object on the table. I lived in this painting for many days.'

Kingcups and Primroses at Llwynhir
Oil, 11 × 11in (27.9 × 27.9cm), 1991

'I often choose a square format and then try to break it in such a way that this is not evident. I think the large area of table-top against the smaller dark background area starts this process and the line of the fold of the cloth and suggestion of a dark shadow on the left helps to carry it on. Nothing of any moment is placed on the centre, but two of the brightest marks, one a cool highlight, the other a warm, pale petal, are on either side and various half-circles play round the centre from further away. Whether these devices are sensed by the spectator, I'm not sure, but they seem important to me when I'm finding them as I look.'

The Park, Narbonne
Drawing, 1987 with Bernard Dunstan on the
near bench.

unlike life, the rectangle on which you are working is static. The visual world is ever changing, but the rectangle is limited, so if I want an equivalent for life within my rectangle, I have to imply and emphasize movement.'

When designing textiles, Diana was very aware of the need for rhythms to lead outwards; in a painting she brings some rhythms back into the frame of the picture.

'I try to set up leading lines and intervals between focal points for the eye to follow around the painting. One of the pleasures of painting is in discovering the emergence of these while working; finding echoes in the set-up between, for example, the curve of a handle opposing the curve of a leaf silhouette, noticing the correspondence of a bright petal shape with a splash of light on the table-cloth, or the pairing of shapes in different subject matter. Some of these discoveries may prove over-dominant or contrary to the original intention of the work and have to be forfeited or modified. If all secondary discoveries serve to enhance and enrich the painting, I know I have touched a creative flow for which I am only partly responsible.

'In nature the negative shape is as beautiful as the positive. It becomes a habit to observe carefully to see the negative shapes made, for example, by the spaces between the leaves or blooms. The "fat" form of a petal does not in nature impinge on the shapes between; they remain correspondingly generous. So often a bad flower painting ignores these shapes, concentrating solely on the leaves and flowers themselves, leaving the negative shapes thin and mean.'

FRESHNESS AND TONALITY

Diana Armfield's flower paintings are remarkable for their freshness; they never appear overworked or laboured and the flowers look as if they had been picked that day (see *The Yellow Pansy*, page 87). Part of her skill in achieving this freshness lies in her ability to get the tones right. Just as she starts her paintings by establishing a linear composition, she also gives herself the tonal massing, placing in areas of light offset by areas of shadow. The watercolourist uses the white paper to suggest light, the oil painter uses the tonal scale. It is the play of warm against cool and light against dark that gives a sense of life in painting. As in landscape, the right tonal balance and contrasts help toward luminous colour. A sunlit field of intense green is suggested in painting not so much by 'pushing' the greens as by finding the precise tone and colour of the areas round it. Likewise a strong red in a flower is not created by adding more and more red pigment, but by playing one red off against another. 'If I look closely at flowers, they teach me this lesson themselves. There are great variations of colour within each flower; what passes for a pink bloom often moves from a cool pink to a warm golden one. Observing these subtle changes which give life to the colour is one of the pleasures of painting flowers.'

Diana Armfield's flowers are often bathed in bright light and the resultant and opposing shadows create not only freshness of colour but also a three-dimensional depth. Sometimes an area will become overworked. She will then scrape across with a palette knife leaving a suggestion of the image beneath. Sometimes a few judicious touches bring all alive again. She may hope that the brushstrokes can stay *alla prima*, but more often than not they will have to be built up further.

'I think the ideal is to get it right the first time, but if I lose that ideal I go for something else. To scrape down after having spent a long time on something does require discipline, but this is part of painting and courage does seem to show in the final painting.

'Too often people paint what they know rather than what they see: if I did this, the results would probably be recognizable but not very interesting. I think concepts are universal, individual observation is unique. Sometimes I

have to continue a painting after the flowers are dead, or when I've left Wales to return to the London studio. Then I have to rely upon my powers of invention and my concepts which I hope are based upon my own observation and memory. Invention is a mixture of knowledge, memory and instinct and is essential to a painter if you are not to fall back on a recipe or formula. Perhaps

Sunday Morning, Luxembourg Gardens, Paris
Watercolour, 9 × 8¾in (22.9 × 22.2cm), 1989

◁ *Roadside Flowers, Northern Spain*
Oil, 9¼ × 8in (23.5 × 20.3cm), 1993

'This bunch was taken from the front of the car to paint in the glass-enclosed balcony of the hotel during a thunderstorm. The light from three sides gave little scope for massing the tones, so instead I did what I could in clustering the colours, also bringing two of the slightly more important flowers together, the daisy and the singing red bloom of the geranium. This had survived from a bunch we made from our own flowers at the beginning of our painting trip, but here, it seems to fit in with the Spanish wild flowers. The orange marigold makes a secondary touch of bright colour to attract the viewer's eye.'

▷ *Flowers on the Christmas Table*
Oil, 10¾ × 11in (27.3 × 27.9cm), 1992

'If there are any flowers or shrubs blooming in our Welsh garden, I like to pick a bunch and paint them over the Christmas days. I had never seen them placed in front of the Christmas cards before. This led me to make a play between the organic forms of the flowers and the flat colours and rectangular shapes of the cards. The more broken and lost edges of the cards prevent them vying for attention, but I think the stalks running across the cards and one of the cast shadows help to link the two. The angles of the stalks are echoed rather more gracefully in their cast shadows on the table.

'This analysis is based rather on hindsight; while painting it would, for the most part, be only semi-conscious, though I do carry on a kind of continuous dialogue in the mind while painting, some of it useful to me, some of it near nonsense.'

The Broad Bean Plant
at Llwynhir
Pencil drawing, 1971

Sometimes people have been puzzled that I find it easier to interpret the translucency of the petals with the opaque medium of oil, rather than with the transparency of watercolour, but translucency can be suggested by getting tones and colours exactly right and this searching for precision of judgment is, for me, enormously satisfying.'

MASTERS AND FOLLOWERS

The most important influence on Diana's development as a painter of flowers was the later work of Allan Gwynne-Jones. 'He revealed a way into painting flowers for me. I had felt that my uncle's approach was the only way and it actually created a barrier. When I saw the later paintings of Allan Gwynne-Jones, I realized that it was something I wanted to do myself.' She is interested in flower painters of the past although few have a direct influence on her work. She greatly admires Manet and the occasional work by Redon. Fantin-Latour she finds interesting, but his work has exerted no real influence. Amongst contemporary painters she admires the sparse paintings of flowers of Euan Uglow which often consist of only one subject, but whose audacity and play of colour she finds fascinating. Many contemporary painters in Britain have been influenced by Diana Armfield's paintings of flowers and she receives letters from artists who have copied her work.

painting is about integrating observation and invention and sometimes I feel as if I'm on a tightrope between the two.'

THE USE OF OIL PAINT

'In my hands watercolour requires a translation as well as an interpretation. I can enjoy this for many subjects which I can see as watercolours, but not yet for flowers. The practice of leaving white paper to act as the lightest tone and the use of transparent washes throughout or contrasted with opaque touches is a very beautiful language, but in trying to interpret the subtleties of flowers in watercolour, I would find the language itself led, instead of my own vision. I have occasionally used pastel for a still life with flowers and found it rewarding, but oil paint is perhaps the most versatile medium and for me the most suited for achieving what I have to say about the subject.

'Imitation is, of course, a form of flattery, and if people feel that they can learn by copying, then I can't object, having learnt from others myself. I find that flowers are lessons in themselves, displaying what I want to explore in painting. They reveal the innate balance and rhythm of life; they display strength and grace and when I paint them I feel I am physically following their curves, but I still have to compose and invent. An initial response is essential; as in all my painting I try to keep the touch direct, and to overwork the touch in painting flowers would seem an impertinence to their special charm.'

THE HIGHGROVE COMMISSION

In September 1988 Diana was asked to go to Highgrove with the prospect of painting two works there.

'Arriving much too early in order not to be late, I was shown into the drawing room to wait for HRH The Prince of Wales. One of his two Jack Russells walked in and settled down in a shaft of sunlight on the carpet; I automatically made a note in my sketch-book, and this was to serve me later. I gazed out of the large front window framed by wisteria, not yet in flower, and recognized the vista which was being carefully planned and indicated by the shrubs and path leading to a "folly" or summer house in the distance. I straightaway decided that I could certainly make something of this view in a painting. Naturally the whole day was memorable for me; the exploring stroll round the various parts of the garden, looking at possible views and also the interesting exchange of ideas on so many of the environmental and conservation issues that I care about and that the Prince of Wales takes up on our behalf. I came away later in the day saying to myself "A man after my own heart, I'm sure I will enjoy painting here." I was especially charmed by the imaginatively conceived kitchen garden, a hint of both France and Italy in a traditional though quite special English walled garden. It was an added pleasure to know that the whole garden is grown organically.

'I had to choose my season, so I decided to forego the nasturtiums spilling over the gravel paths and the climbing roses rampant over the pergolas, to return in the spring. I had in mind the fruit blossom seen against the brick walls and the interesting white gates. The first day I arrived with my box, an umbrella fixed to a wheel basket against possible rain, and various panels to paint on. The blossom was not quite ready, but this proved useful as I could see through the branches and tight buds of an apple tree to the gate I had chosen to include. I was able to make

notes but spent most of the day on a view out of the drawing room window, having first asked for a large drugget to cover the carpet. I also requested that the pretty china service, from which I had been given coffee, should be placed on a table by the window to be included as part of the interior, softening the corner of the window [see *View out of the Drawing Room Window*, page 75].

'I have to thank the staff at Highgrove for some second-sight tact. That first day's effort was quite appalling but none of them came to look before I had packed it away. I took the panel back to my studio and over the weekend made a fresh start on another board; it was not information but touch that had gone awry, and of course I blamed the ground of the board and the brushes. I returned with the new, much better start and there were the staff all about, full of interest and appreciation for the proceedings. There was no little Jack Russell to be seen but I had my sketch-book note. I wanted the dog on the window seat, so I placed a china parrot as a "stand in" for the tone and colour of the shadow. On later visits the blossom was out in the kitchen garden and filling up the view, but I had my "start" and could add blossom where I thought I needed it. I spent several rewarding days painting in and about the kitchen garden; in fact two paintings became four as new ideas developed, and I wanted to give the Prince of Wales some choice [see *Kitchen Garden in April*, page 74].

'There were surprise episodes before the paintings were finished. I came along one morning to get on with a view of the house seen through an arched gateway only to find a cement mixer occupying the space and most of the surround to the gate demolished; curiously as the "unfinished" painting stayed in the studio it finished itself with the aid of a couple of brush strokes. This can happen occasionally. In all I did four paintings and was delighted that all were accepted. I spent my last moments picking a beautiful bunch of wild flowers from the meadow from which I painted a still life on my return to the studio.' (See *Wild Flowers from Highgrove Meadow*, page 74.)

△ *Wild Flowers from Highgrove Meadow*
Oil, 14¼ × 10¼ (36.2 × 26cm), 1989

While Diana was working on the Highgrove commission, the Prince of Wales told her to pick
whatever flowers she liked from the meadow. On
her last day of work she went into the meadow,
which was full of wild flowers, and gathered a bunch
which she painted in Kew.

She often likes to use two vases or glasses rather
than one to give rhythm and interaction between
forms. The '*prima donna*' is the dandelion with its
supporting buttercups which are set off by the
purples, blues and violets of the other flowers. The
broken, free brushwork keeps the painted surface
alive and vital, while the build-up of different layers

of colours provides an intriguing richness and depth.
It is a painting to be contemplated over a period of
time, and only through contemplation will its
richness and complexity be fully revealed.

△ *Kitchen Garden in April, Highgrove*
Oil, 9 × 9in (22.9 × 22.9cm), 1989

View out of the Drawing Room Window,
Highgrove
Oil, 14 × 12in (35.6 × 30.5cm), 1989

5

WORKING IN OILS

Diana Armfield finds that the particular quality of the support influences the outcome of the painting more than most people realize. When she says 'I like to have started before I start' she is stressing a need to work on a sympathetic surface in both texture and colour. The toned panel itself can give the underlying note of the painting, particularly if she succeeds in allowing the colour of the toned ground to play a part. She draws a parallel to Sickert's description of his way of painting: like strewing cards on a green baize table, allowing each successive layer of touches to play a part. Her primed, toned board stands for the green baize table.

PREPARING THE SUPPORT

Diana uses hardboard or mounting board as her basic support, over which she stretches fine cotton. Occasionally she works on a canvas; this has quite a different 'feel'. Hardboard is used for larger panels, but mounting board is light and ideally suited for painting trips abroad, for working on the spot.

'Either I or Bernard, and mostly Bernard, will make up a batch of panels at a time by sizing fine cotton on to the boards using real rabbit-skin size. We use old worn-out cotton or linen sheets. The boards are then prepared with a home-made emulsion made by mixing egg, water and linseed oil together, added to titanium white powder and finally letting down with warm rabbit-skin size. I have to find out for myself the exact amount of absorbency I want for the support; the more size added to the emulsion the less absorbent the surface will be. By trial and error I hope to achieve the surface I want and this may vary according to the demands of the subject.

Vines near Limoux, France

Sketch-book drawing for a painting, 1986

'One work I may see in terms of rather flat matt shapes for which an absorbent surface would seem ideal. Alternatively I might want to keep the paint very fluid, easily pushed about, with an element of the linear, and then a far less absorbent ground would be appropriate. In fact I find that it mostly works the other way round. I choose a board which I think is right in size, proportion and colour and I have to accept the surface as it comes. If it is rather absorbent I probably curse but find myself adapting the way I put the paint on. I may perhaps enjoy the flatter, more matt feel, but if I don't, there is always the hope that the paint I am putting on today will make for a less absorbent surface for tomorrow; one which will take subsequent touches more freely. On the other hand, if the panel proves very non-absorbent, the first day's touches will probably not cover the toned ground even where I want them to, and the brush marks will be slipping about, the paint dribbling down. This might be all right, but could be exasperating if I had intended solid touches, which on the ideal panel could have been left *alla prima*. However, once again, the panel will improve for the next day once it has some paint on it. These examples show how much the final result may be influenced by the support.

'I like an active surface on which to begin. Sometimes I tone the board with the mixtures on the palette left after a day's painting, but more often I take a rag and rub in one of the earth colours adding touches of other pigments to break up the colour. I like to end up with a variety of toned boards to choose from, some with variations of honey colour or warm brown, others more grey-blue, grey-violet or grey-green. I haven't tried to paint on a white panel for many years and for work outside it would be too dazzling. Perhaps even more important, I find it easier to work from a middle tone down towards the darks and up towards the lights. If I started on a white ground I should have the quite considerable problem of relating all the tones to the one extreme.

'At the beginning of a painting trip there will be a good number of panels to choose from. By the end, if the weather has been kind, we will be "making do" from the few that are left. The toned ground can either be a foil to the dominant colour of the scene, or one in which the colour can be left untouched to play a conspicuous part in the painting. Both can be rewarding and the choice is largely instinctive. If I do use the ground colour as a foil, for example a honey coloured panel on which to play the blues and violets of a sky and bright greens of foliage, I hope to find that this opposition of warm and cool will help me achieve certain luminous vibrations between one colour and another.

'Grounds made for the purpose will inevitably be rather smooth, even if the rub-in of oil paint is left with brush or rag marks, and for the most part they will answer my needs very well, but an old failed painting can make an ideal surface. One of the consolations of having wrecked a painting is knowing that in due time, when it has thoroughly dried out – at least a year – the failure will make a delicious support. The very fact that I have to obliterate the subject matter underneath, though not necessarily all the surface of the original painting, makes me work with decision, and the actual brush strokes seem to go on extra sweetly. For a larger work on canvas, perhaps because there is the "tooth" of the canvas to work against, I don't feel the need of anything but a rather light-toned ground, and this usually results in higher keyed colour throughout. I don't often use failed canvases because as soon as they are off their stretchers they look and feel like old linoleum.'

THE ACT OF PAINTING

'The approach to painting, both physical and mental, naturally varies. A sketch on the spot seems to call out for solid touches which ideally can be left *alla prima*. This is, of course, a counsel of perfection, but it is in the nature of

The Ocean, Cottesloe Beach, Western Australia
Oil, 3¼ × 6½in (8.2 × 16.5cm), 1985

'Our time in Australia coincided with temperatures of over 100 degrees. Most days, after the afternoon sessions at the art school were over, we got down to the beach for me to bathe and paint for an hour; sunset came very quickly and was quite sudden. This oil sketch was done on a bit of sized wood, which helped me to get something of the drama of contrast between the deep, dark sea of the horizon coming up to the turquoise of the shallow water and golden sand.'

△ *Vines in Italy*
Oil, 8 × 6¼in (20.3 × 15.8cm), 1989

A lively oil sketch completed on the spot, it relates to the larger oils of vines in Italy (pages 2 and 38). Notice how important a role the underpainting plays in the overall tonality, providing both a foil to the blues and greens and a unifying element underlying the whole panel.

△ *Cat on the Giudecca, Venice*
Oil, 8½ × 9in (21.6 × 22.9cm), 1992

A delightful and unusual view of Venice. The Giudecca lies across the lagoon from San Marco and is rarely visited by tourists; the church of San Giorgio Maggiore is seen here from the side. The artist has used the strong shadows in the foreground to compose the painting, creating a subtle play of pinks, light-blue violets and the warm terracotta of the Venetian bricks. Into this framework she has placed her figures, themselves half in sunlight, half in shade, seen walking towards us at a leisurely pace. The cat provides a charming focal point, which works both as a compositional device and as a reminder that Venice also has its peaceful backwaters.

On the Riva, Venice
Sketch-book drawing for
a painting, 1981

'The more considered work is likely to develop from a start in which I begin with thinner paint, building up to more solid paint in specific lighter areas. There may be quite conscious contrasting of areas of thin paint against quite heavy impasto; I'm still hoping that parts of the toned ground will remain and act as a foil to both. But this is assuming that a painting goes according to a plan, which it doesn't, and only too often a cherished bit of toned ground gets overlaid in the pursuance of getting something else right.

'I like to paint standing well back from the easel so that I am using the whole arm and not just the wrist or fingers. I played tennis for many years and I sometimes think that the act of painting can be likened to the good tennis stroke, controlled freedom of movement resulting in absolute precision. I fail just about as often as I did in a game of tennis. I sometimes find that if difficulties arise I get nearer and nearer the easel without noticing; this begins to show as tension in the work. I then force myself to stand back or sit in a comfortable chair and contemplate the work from a distance; contemplation is an important part of painting, and, as Vuillard said, the armchair is an important feature in the studio.

'I often start a painting in the studio using rather fluid paint, in a colour which is not taken from the local colour of the scene, very often blue. This is really to give me the main directions, rhythms and divisions on which to build. Most of this drawing will get obliterated by subsequent touches but some of it may remain if needed. On the spot I sometimes give myself a touch or two of the darkest and lightest element in the scene to act as points of reference to all the other tones. I don't always stand to paint on the spot; there is not always the space or the time to put up the easel and in Venice especially I feel less conspicuous sitting on a camp stool. The drawbacks of sitting are obvious; it is difficult not to crouch, as the hours go by, so there is inevitably the occupational hazard of backache. I'm not good at stopping nearly often enough to get up,

a sketch that it is based on one intense response to the subject carried through quickly in one go. It is exhilarating to paint a sketch and I hope that this gets translated into the result, which is usually more obviously a success or calamity than more considered work painted in the studio, or the more thought-out paintings executed on the spot. One of the virtues of the sketch is that it is done without any thought of showing the result in an exhibition. I do sketches because I must: something, usually of an ephemeral nature, often to do with some special effect of light, has called out to me. I start without deliberation and with only a little care as to whether it will compose or not. Afterwards a few prove to have "worked", and these do get framed, shown and perhaps give particular pleasure. I rather think that if I thought of them as exhibition works beforehand, they would become commonplace.

step back and look at what I am doing, and there is the temptation to use the wrist and fingers rather than the whole arm, especially when dealing with the smaller forms.'

COLOURS AND MARKS

Diana has a huge range of colours on her palette, although she is unlikely to use them all in one painting. Her palette comprises flake white (titanium being too cold and all-pervading), Naples yellow, cadmium yellow, yellow ochre, raw sienna, cadmium red, light red, alizarin crimson, permanent rose (often used in a still life of flowers), Indian red, burnt sienna or Venetian red, raw umber, Bohemian green earth, terre verte, viridian, emerald, cobalt, violet light, and either ivory-black or blue-black. She uses four blues: cerulean which she often uses for the initial drawing, cobalt, royal and ultramarine. She uses black, sometimes for mixing with burnt sienna or other warm earth colours to produce greys. In fact most of her colours she uses mixed, rarely finding that the colour in the tubes is exactly what she wants. Working in the studio she lays out her colours along the edge of the palette, leaving the whole area in front for mixing. Anything left at the end of the day from this mixing area is taken off and the palette almost polished with turps or medium so that over the years it develops a nice surface on which to mix the colours. Only the dried-up colours are removed from their places around the back edge of the palette. With the passing of time this has become a 'mountain range' of paint and the palette far too heavy to hold. On painting trips she makes an effort to prevent the paint building up in this way to avoid carrying unnecessary weight. The colours are ranged methodically from left to right, from white to yellows through the ochres, reds and browns on to the cooler violets and then blues, greens and finally black. This gives the spectrum from warm to cool and from light to dark, at a glance.

Most artists' use of colour is a personal and often intuitive process, not based upon scientific or even methodical formulae. Diana Armfield has looked closely at, and benefited from, the work of artists from the past.

'Lurking at the back of my mind I retain the theory that the dark colours seem most intense and luminous if they are kept lean, but that whites and the paler earth colours can be most enjoyed when built up into a much thicker impasto; that they may even look meagre if put on too lean. This is the theory and practice of the Old Masters, Reynolds, Rembrandt and Gainsborough. They kept the darks lean, used glazes and built up the lights with much thicker paint. Of course that is a very different practice from the Impressionist use of touches and small areas of solid paint, light or dark patches, one against the other. How it comes out is what matters. One does not always want an intense luminous dark, nor a build-up of an impasto; dead dark areas can be quite strange, beautiful and appropriate; lean whites have their place too. However, the Old Masters' theory and practice does make me hesitate before attempting to get something darker by putting on another touch of something even darker on top, without first passing the palette knife over the paint.

'For me, mixing paint is an entirely empirical process. I

Below Les Baux, Provence
Sketch-book note, 1979

note below les Baux.

Umbrellas Up, Venice
Oil, 9½ × 7½in (24.2 × 19.1cm), 1990

Once again Diana has sought out an unusual aspect of Venice – the city depicted during a winter rainstorm. This is a marvellous piece of tonal painting, the colours restricted to a narrow range of greys, umbers and just a hint of burnt sienna, all set off by the rich blacks of the umbrellas and raincoats. It is also a fascinating composition with the firmly handled architectural elements to the right acting as an anchor to the fluidity of the wet pavement. The focal point of the picture, the figures with their umbrellas, appears more than half way up the composition. It is, above all, an atmospheric painting capturing a moment and a feeling of 'place' which the artist so effectively communicates to her viewers.

Dusk in the Piazzetta, Venice
Oil, 15¾ × 13¼in (39.9 × 33.6cm), 1993

'This was done entirely in the studio from a drawing and the memory of the luminous blue sky playing against the patches of reflection in the pavement. I often watch and make notes of the people in the Piazzetta, how parts of them are clear against dark or light, while the rest of them is lost. The pale blobs made by the lights relate to the stream of dark heads, nicely interrupted by the white hat. The lady with the striped jacket was a gift, so also the child in her white top and dark leggings.'

The Tethered Goat,
France
Oil, 15½ × 19¾in (39.4 × 50.2cm), 1984

what I observe is far more important to me than theories about colour. This does not prevent me from theorizing myself and talking to Bernard about them. When we are both in for lunch we usually chatter about painting, and when we are in the car together, we often comment on some effect of light on the landscape saying "How would you get that colour, how do you see it?" Frost on the landscape, producing as it does the most exquisite, varied and indefinable colour, as it half conceals the grass or bracken in shadow or light, will surely prompt such talk. I doubt whether the next time I am actually painting the frost, it will look at all the same, nor will I remember what mixture either of us conjured up in our minds, but such talk clarifies the delights of observing.'

put my brush into any pigment on the palette that will help me achieve the colour I want. There is, I suppose, a certain pleasure in achieving it immediately, using only two or three, but getting it right against another colour, rather than how I achieve it, is what I am conscious of. When I buy a tube of colour that I've not come across before, I probably think it is going to be quite special, the answer for all kinds of equivalents. For a few weeks it will be tried in all sorts of mixtures. A very few of these become permanent additions to my palette. Most remain to harden on my painting table for years to come.

'I was aware from childhood that my uncle Maxwell Armfield based his colour relationships on both musical and certain esoteric theories; he found a close link between musical and colour scales and he related both to the Fibonacci series. I find the colour relationships in his work, mostly tempera, not only exquisite but also true and often surprising. I could not follow him in these theories, which served him so well, fascinating though they are, but no doubt they have left their mark on me, and his work tells of the power and subtlety produced by one finely adjusted colour seen against another. I have to develop my awareness of colour relationships from looking at nature;

She has a wide range of brushes, mostly hog-hair filberts of differing sizes, although she also uses some round brushes, but rarely flats. She finds that hog-hair brushes allow the paint to breathe, and finds sables too smooth, even 'slimy'. However she uses a small sable to sign her work and occasionally finds herself carrying on with the painting with the signing brush, adding final touches.

'I am always on the look-out for good brushes and never go past an art shop without going in to see if one amongst their stock looks and feels good. A good hog-hair brush has a perfect combination of spring and silkiness. In the past the hogs' hair was selected by hand but today most brushes are mechanically made and the bristles heat-treated to curve inwards. As a result some of the bristles quickly uncurl. I do not use nylon brushes as I find them flaccid.

'The language of painting interests me as much as the subject, or rather the two depend on each other. The actual handling, the touch, is part of this language. I want the brush stroke to explain objects and at the same time create part of the abstract life of the painting. Moving away from making flat areas of colour in textiles to painting, I became conscious of the brush stroke or mark made with a palette knife as part of that language. It is this duality of purpose that fascinates me in painting. I sometimes think of this abstract structure as working rather like a house built of cards, but cards of differing sizes, shapes, colours and tones all contributing towards an equilibrium of all the dynamic directions, curves and divisions that make up a painting.

'I admire the role of the brush stroke in Chinese and Japanese art; nothing could be more beautiful than their interpretations of bamboos, flowers and birds; the way in which they show us the markings on a bird, finding, apparently without effort, an equivalent to the rhythms before them, and revealing both the strength and elegance of the subject. I respond even more to Turner's language, especially in his watercolours. His studies of birds and fish, and his views of Venice, give us both universal rhythms of life and at the same time reveal the individuality of the subject. This, I think, suits my Western mind.'

TONALITY AND COMPOSITION

Diana Armfield does not consider herself to be a natural tonal painter. 'As a result of my textile training, my painting is based on colour relationship within a narrow tonal range. Much of my painting is based on the playing of warm colours against cool and it is in this way that I try to achieve luminosity. A true tonal painter, for example Ken Howard, uses much less range of colour than I do, but has a far wider tonal range. I am interested and delighted to find in some of his beach scenes, where the figures are seen against the light, that he manages to imply colour, so that one knows that a particular figure was actually wearing red or blue, but there is no red or blue in the painting. In my own work I take special pleasure in succeeding with implied colour; painting a shirt in just the right tone of blue or violet which to the spectator is clearly seen as a white shirt in shadow. Bernard always takes

photographs of my finished pictures along with his own; these tend to show up more tonal contrast than actually exists in the painting. When I look at the photographs I sometimes wish that I had actually achieved as much in the painting.'

Many of Diana's landscape and townscape paintings are executed in the studio from drawings done on the spot or developed from small oil panels begun likewise on site. She finds that working from drawings makes her concentrate more upon the geometry of composition.

'In the studio I am conscious of making geometrical relationships between the various elements within the painting. For instance, I am very conscious of how I place the people, pigeons, dogs and patterns of paving to form certain links together, and all these to the architecture and the actual rectangle of the panel. Working on the spot I hope that I arrive at geometry by instinct and observation. When first caught by a scene, at that moment when one

Vines along the Road to the Farm
CarbOthello pencil on Canson paper for small oil, 1979

△ **Summer Flowers at Llwynhir**
Oil, 12¼ × 10½in (31.1 × 26.8cm), 1989

The dominant bloom in this flower painting is the translucent pink rose whose full shape is reflected in the nasturtium leaf next to it. They are supported by the fresh reds, yellows and blues of the flowers behind. The folds in the table-cloth, the edge of the table and the darker furniture behind give the composition a structure which is broken by the exuberant painting of the flowers. Again the apparently free brushwork keeps the paint quality fresh and prevents it from appearing overworked.

◁ *Campo San Giacomo dell'Orio, Venice*
Oil, 11 × 8in (27.9 × 20.3cm), 1993

'There are *campi* in Venice that I gravitate towards and make my own; others, rather austere, usually empty, I and evidently others walk through quickly, although the architecture may be just as impressive.

'This one is the right size, has more than one bench to choose from, and is nearly always animated by people talking, children and dogs.

'It isn't the easiest *campo* to find or to compose; the trees are splendid but isolated. I shifted myself a few yards this way and that before feeling quite sure that I had something. The two figures on the left arrived while I was looking and wondering, one in a striped jersey. With them and the other figures, the dog and the child half lost in the shadow, I began to see how I could compose the painting. The arrival of the figure wearing the striped jersey was a stroke of luck.'

◁ *Summer Roses in Wales*
Oil, 10¾ × 8¼in (27.3 × 20.9cm), 1992

A delightfully simple and direct painting in which the intense pink of the rose is set against the light table-cloth. Notice how the underpainting of the board is allowed to show through in the glass providing both visual interest and depth. The subtle blues and violets of the shadows 'sing' against the rich pinks and greens of the flowers and leaves.

▷ *The Yellow Pansy*
Oil, 9¼ × 5¼in (23.5 × 13.3cm), 1991

'I had been given the little white antique jug as a present, so wanted to paint something in it immediately and in the simplest way, but there were really only these flowers available in the garden. It often proves difficult to manage strong red and yellow together in one painting, though I'm sure Bonnard often delighted in putting them side by side. I can find that they look harsh and unattractive, and usually avoid the combination both in painting and in the garden. So this painting, which I more or less completed in a couple of hours, became a play between two different yellows and two, even three, reds. Where the two colours really touch, the shadowed area of the yellow pansy becomes modified, which I think reconciles it to the deep red polyanthus, which itself shifts towards crimson. The quite dominant counterchange in the two blooms – dark on light against light on dark – adds another theme to the painting.'

Buffet Lunch on the QE2

Drawing on Canson paper for a pastel, 1991

extra help in drawing to a foreign student. He was in despair because, however full the form in front of him, his drawings appeared flat. I remember holding up for him a circular piece of flat cardboard and an orange and asking him to compare the edges all round first of the flat cardboard and then of the orange. I think I learnt as much as he did from that lesson. Since painting I delight in the subtleties of edge, the delicious "lost and found" quality that life in the solid exhibits. Degas and Toulouse-Lautrec and in our own time Allan Gwynne-Jones and Peter Greenham, all deliciously revealed this particular aspect of visual appearance.'

Diana is wary of photographs as a working tool for the painter.

'Artists who rely on photographs often end up with black shadows and obvious solutions. The photograph tends to wash out the strong sunlit areas and darken the shadows, so losing the tonal variations. I think an artist should try to use his own eyes to sort out what is going on in a scene. If I stand and draw or paint on the spot I know that I nourish my visual memory as well as absorbing new relationships of colour and tone. By looking intently I learn far more than by taking a photograph. I do use photographs to help with certain specific objects when my drawing proves inadequate, but often I find that the very things I've noticed seem insignificant in the photograph. One day in the Campo in Siena I sat in a café and drew one of the small ways leading off. I saw as interesting and important the shapes of the signs, drainpipes and gutters standing out from the walls, and when I had finished I took a photograph. When I got the photograph back I was surprised to see that all the signs and drainpipes had been reduced to insignificance, whereas to my eyes their odd shapes dominating the scene were my very reason for choosing the view. Of course I do use photographs as *aides-mémoire*, especially if I am doing a commission, but that is

says "I want to make something of that", I think one's innate artistry has seen at a glance a whole series of relationships that offer what satisfies at the deepest level. Artists both see and want different visual relationships. In life we all need different amounts of sleep, stimulation, complexity and simplicity, wit, surprise and stability. I think this is reflected in what we choose to paint, and, when we work from imagination or drawings, how we compose.

'It is sometimes pointed out to me that I clearly enjoy a sense of recession in painting, so I suppose whenever I come across such subject matter – sunset paths across water, vistas leading away to beyond – I readily see possibilities that I want to paint. I grew up by the edge of the New Forest and from the windows of our house we could see the blue hills of Dorset which beckoned for walks at weekends on the chalk downs, springy turf and fresh aromatic air. I dare say my enjoyment of recession in painting has something to do with those early pleasures.

'While I was still a designer it was natural to draw the shapes of my motifs with distinct edges all round because this does, of course, imply flatness, which is what I wanted. Even my studies of natural forms reflected this attitude. While I was still a designer, I was asked to give largely nerves! However, when I'm painting I keep them well away from the easel. I also find that photography is essential for keeping a record of every piece of work I do. Sometimes these photographs show the unexpected, either some passage that was resolved in the wrong way, or may suggest something that could be developed further, and I may then be tempted to adjust the painting.'

Training a visual memory is important to Diana Armfield as she believes that it is essential for a painter who works in the studio from drawings. 'Unfortunately I was not blessed with a good visual memory but by drawing regularly I have been able more or less to train it. When I draw direct I absorb much more than I realize. Later, when I look at the drawings I remember the heat or cold, the perfume of the landscape and the weather. I can remember so much about a view or a landscape from looking at a drawing.' These form the basis of Diana's studio work and she keeps all her sketch-books which go back many years, sometimes working on an oil or a pastel from a sketch made many years earlier.

She likes to look long at a subject before beginning to work.

'The ideal on a painting trip abroad is to find the perfect picnic place: shade which will last, shelter from wind, no troublesome noise, congenial passers-by or none, a flat space for two chairs, all overlooking the scene I am going to paint. I gaze at this chosen view all through the picnic. By the end of the meal the urge to get going will be quite intense. I think that I know what I am going to do and will visualize it on the panel. Of course I push the paint around and need to keep rethinking, but oil paint is an adaptable medium, allowing me to scrape down, change, adjust and repaint. When we are on a painting trip I start a journal as I find it helpful to re-read the relevant pages before I begin a painting.'

FRAMING

Diana Armfield allows her paintings to dry out for about nine months before applying a first coat of varnish, followed the next day with a wax varnish which takes the shine off the picture varnish. The painting will then go to the framer's where important decisions are taken.

'As most of my oil paintings are small, I take great care over the frames; the two will be seen as one whole. I started with J. T. Burns in Emerald Street; later he took on the framing business at the Royal Academy, from which he has now retired. The times spent with him choosing from his mouldings were an education. It was a morning's work, often ending with lunch at a local Italian restaurant. It took so long because as each new client came through the door, Terry would abandon the previous customer to deal with the newcomer. Sometimes there would be six of us all vying for his attention. To avoid too much frustration, some of us would join in on the choice of mouldings for others. I'm sure we gained experience in this way; we often met old friends and made many new acquaintances. Later his charming wife, Sue, took a part and quietly resolved problems. Terry was immensely generous to his artist customers, giving us off-cuts of mounting board and advising us with "tricks of the trade". The relationship with a framer has to be one of sympathy and confidence. I now go to C. D. Soar in Launceston Place where I discuss with David Cavaghan or Michael Beddowes the frame for each painting in turn, and the atmosphere is a good deal calmer than it ever was in Emerald Street. It is inevitable that every now and then the finish of the frame will be found to be not quite suitable for the painting. When this happened at Emerald Street, I seldom had the courage to ask for it to be altered; I took it home and asked Bernard to alter it, or had a go myself. At C. D. Soar I actually benefit, as their reworking of a finish nearly always means increased richness and subtlety.'

▷ *Buffet Lunch on the QE2*
Pastel, 7¼ × 10¾in (18.4 × 27.3cm), 1991

'There are people of all ages and all kinds on the QE2, and the temptation to pile the plate from the buffet was not easily resisted, especially by the young person who kept her hat on. She sat next to her father, who had pinned badges all over his beret, and they made an irresistible pair. Another time I would hope to make more of the many interesting profiles of those figures silhouetted against the window, but this time I was engrossed with the duo in the foreground and the complicated overlapping of glasses and crockery on the table.'

△ *Below San Gimignano – The Lady in Green*
Oil, 7¼ × 9¾in (19.7 × 24.8cm), 1993

'This is the favourite path below the ramparts where people walk their dogs in the late afternoon. The scene composes into a sweeping rhythm right across. The dappled tree trunks reminded me of Gerard Manley Hopkins' poem *Pied Beauty* on "dappled things", but I could only recall a couple of lines. I specially enjoyed the green of the lady's jacket with her red shoulder bag against the very different greens of the foliage.'

▷ *The Deck Café on the QE2*
Pastel, 6½ × 5¾in (16.5 × 14.5cm), 1989

A luminous pastel bathed in a clear summer Atlantic light. The buff-coloured Canson paper is used as a foil to the pale blue light of the sky, while the darker blue of the parasols provides an element of visual excitement.

6

WORKING ON PAPER

THE ROLE OF DRAWING

Drawing underlies Diana Armfield's art and she stresses the importance of recording her experiences on paper.

Fondamenta Ognissanti, Venice
Sketch-book drawing for an etching, 1992

'I would like to draw every day, but it doesn't always happen. When I taught at the Byam Shaw Art School I urged the students to record in their sketch-books all that they did, including the simplest of activities, getting up in the morning, the view from their window, what they saw on the way to college. I did this because I found that, having grown out of "child art" which does encompass both the familiar world and fantasy, the students mostly arrived rather limited in their responses to the visual world. Many of them only opened their eyes when they walked through the doors of the college studios, or when shown what was worth looking at by a tutor. I think that partly because I was teaching, I myself found almost everything in the visual world a possible source of material from which to work.

'Since that time I realize that my own responses have narrowed down. I now only want to work from what enhances life for me. Fortunately this is still quite a wide world and for me a changing one. Over the years I have got more interested in drawing and painting the people who inhabit my scenes, and while I'm working I watch with interest or invent situations, relationships, conversations between them in a way that I don't think I did a few years ago. This was probably because it seemed difficult enough to get the figures to fit convincingly enough into the work at all, even to look human and the right size. Even now the people in my scenes are sometimes obliged to change from man to woman, elegant to stout, or any other transformation, because one touch of the pastel has lost the first idea and turned a promising young woman into an oaf. On the other hand I am often surprised and comforted by finding that just because I am thinking myself into the scene as being in Venice, America or Fortnum's, the people do end up appropriately belonging.

'Most of my drawing is done away from the studio on our painting trips, and it must be assumed that we are in places which we enjoy exploring. Everything is on offer and I will pause to draw on every possible occasion. It is difficult to cross the Piazza San Marco in Venice without wanting to make a note of some apparently new effect of light or the fog on the façade of the church or the campanile; or being caught by some small part of the whole scene. I choose a subject either because I'm enjoying the scene and think I can compose it or because I can see something which might come in useful at a later stage; people talking in a group; the pigeons, dogs or cats. Sometimes I just sit with my sketch-book to hand watching the scene for something good to turn up. This is a delightful way of idling profitably and suits very well if I've been working at something for some hours and want a break. I am always attracted by particular effects of light or the way shadows fall. These are usually line drawings with written notes about tones or colour. In the past I used to produce more detailed drawings, sometimes giving the tones a series of numbers to grade their depth. Nowadays I am less methodical, relying more upon my visual memory and on my journal which I write up each night, recording what has happened during the day, including comments and observations about anything and anybody, rewarding times and disasters, the latter being more amusing to read later than experienced at the time.

'When we go on our painting trips abroad I can't be content until I've "opened the score" with a drawing of some sort. The first drawings, after a day or two spent packing up and travelling, may be tentative or clumsy but they start the flow going. When I look at them all on our return I can see that they do become more fluent as the days pass. However, first drawings are not necessarily less

Volterra
Sketch-book drawing for
a pastel, 1991

Ladies at Lunch, Fortnum's
Pastel, 9¼ × 10½in (23.5 × 26.8cm), 1991

On page 44 Diana Armfield discusses her enjoyment of drawing in the restaurant at Fortnum and Mason. Our eyes are led over the foreground napkins, table-cloth and glasses towards the central group of ladies who appear engrossed in their meal. They are all wearing hats, which feature in the composition and are offset by the waitress in black and white. The painting of elephants by David Shepherd which hangs behind the group acts as a 'painting within a painting', as well as providing an amusing contrast of subject matter.

Deciding on the Menu, Plaza Tea Room, New York
Pastel, 9¼ × 8in (23.5 × 20.3cm), 1992

'We have made drawings in this opulent tea room on more than one occasion. This time I had intended to make more of the splendid carpet and chandeliers than the people, but the lady in black and white was obviously the focus of attention. She was too good to pass over. I was lucky; there was an almighty thunderstorm while we were there and people stayed put drinking tea, instead of removing themselves as they often do just as I'm putting pencil to paper.'

useful; it is really the information I am after even though it is obviously more enjoyable to work later from an expressive drawing.

'I don't draw well standing up holding my sketch-book; I simply lose control of the pencil, so I carry about a light camp stool and a cushion. However, many views are seen best when standing up, so I am often obliged to compromise. I like to spend up to an hour drawing and contemplating before moving on. If the weather is possible, I will have my box with me and at least some of the days will be spent on oil sketches, or a painting of more importance. I hope to go home with both a full sketch-book and a number of oil sketches which will remind me of the light and colour, the "note" of that particular trip.

'At the Slade I thought of myself as a poor draughtsman; others, particularly Bernard, were far more gifted. I think I was slow to benefit from the teaching; the elegant explanatory notes, drawn by Randolph Schwabe on the top right-hand corner of my cartridge paper, meant little to me; I can be very stupid. On an early trip to Venice I learnt something about drawing which was immensely valuable to me for later sketch-book notes. I was trying to draw the complicated façade of San Marco and making a hash of it. Whenever I took my eyes off the scene to look at what I had done, I promptly lost my place. In some despair I gave up bothering about what was happening on the page; instead I kept my eyes and mind on the façade. My pencil followed what my eyes were telling me; I didn't look down until I had done all I could. The result surprised me. There on the paper was an expressive drawing showing clearly all the emphases I had felt. Although the verticals and horizontals were rather drunken-looking, the drawing meant what I had seen and was also more useful. Of course this is no recipe; the drawing can only be as good as what the eye sees and makes sense of. If I can't look intelligently and with purpose, the drawing will make that quite clear as well.'

DRAWINGS FOR DIFFERENT PURPOSES

'Drawing is a way of noting down information, a way of responding to a subject, and sometimes for thinking out the composition of the work. I do a great deal from the pencil drawings in my sketch-book, but part of my purpose in doing them is to make sure that I am spending time looking and absorbing as much about the scene as possible. These drawings are largely instinctive responses to the subject. I also make more complete drawings which might take one or two mornings to produce. On a Venice trip, if it's raining, I may go into San Marco and spend time there drawing on Canson paper using a white and a brown CarbOthello pencil. I use these two pencils of different tones simply because I'm going to find it difficult to see what I'm doing in that dark interior. I try to put down as precisely as possible where the divisions come in the architecture and move from the big forms on towards the smaller ones made up by the lights, the lamps and the decoration. These drawings often form the basis for pastels worked on later in the studio, so I will be visualizing a pastel as I draw. I find magic in the dark mysterious atmosphere, the crimson lights glowing from the opulent hanging lamps, the glints of richness coming from out of the misty purple haze, the touch of scarlet at the altar. People come in, pause to gaze up at the mosaics in the domed ceilings; a few stay to pray and then move on. I note some of them down, but may move them about when I come to work on the pastel [see *Interior of San Marco*, page 11].

'On one occasion, a dark overcast day, I was deep in my drawing, I had thought unnoticed. Suddenly all round me was illuminated. A verger approached me with the sweetest smile. He indicated by a gesture that he had noticed me struggling to see, so had ordered all the lights to be put on until I had finished. Thus he killed my drawing with kindness!

'Not all these drawings come to anything, but I seldom

discard them. They may lie about the studio for months, hence the growing piles, until there is a wholesale clear-out. I think perhaps few women easily tolerate waste. I even keep faulty mounts and at idle moments place one or another round one of those drawings. Quite often I find that a little portion makes something that works on its own, or perhaps the mount shows me what I can do to develop the work into something more satisfying. I like to be taken back in imagination to the scene. This, after all, is one of the real pleasures of working from drawings in the studio, something that abstract painters cannot experience.

'I also draw outside, making studies which are ends in themselves. Most of these are done in Wales or the Rockies of America where, every other year, we spend some weeks with our youngest son, Bob, and his family. Again I mostly use CarbOthello pencils on Canson paper. In Wales it is the landscape with the sheep that invites me, and in the Rockies the tantalizing aspen trees in the landscape. These drawings are often about finding connections between one thing and another in the scene. For example, I might be interested in where an angle of light on a tree trunk leads my eye or the connection between branches of an aspen tree and the rocks behind. I have long admired John Flavin's drawings. To me they appear based on a rigorous searching out of these connecting rhythms; they are wonderfully precise yet delicious under his touch. The drawings suggest the rocks, the lie of the land, the dried grasses, but the clue to the subject matter is given only by these connections; the drawings are anything but explicit and quite beautiful. I find for myself I have to develop the drawing to a point where at least some of the subject matter begins to explain itself, but I attempt to do this without losing any of the relationships. It is discovering these connections and putting them down that I find is the fascination of drawing in this way. Occasionally I add touches of pastel to these drawings, but it is sometimes a mistake.

'The sheep round us in Wales are a timid lot, and I have to be very alert to get something down before they make off [see *Sheep up the Bank*, page 51]. Later, at my leisure, I can carry on with the drawing of the trees and hedges. I'm really using a lot of invention, but the scene I'm drawing gradually becomes quite real to me. Months later I'm not sure how much was there and how much I've invented.'

DRAWING WITH SOFT PASTELS

Working in pastels requires organization and Diana Armfield finds it an unsuitable medium for working on the spot.

'There are practical problems with working in pastels on the spot; my hands get dirty from holding the pastels, the paper is easily smudged, and there is the main problem of having the wrong colours with me. I work in pastel in the

People in the Impressionist Gallery at the Metropolitan Museum, New York
Sketch-book note, 1989

◁ *The Straw Hat, Venice*

Pastel, 9½ × 9½in (24.2 × 24.2cm), 1992

'After working all morning, and a picnic lunch with Bernard on the Zattere, I like to stroll slowly back to the hotel, exploring and making notes in my sketch-book of anything that offers itself. I passed this scene of a late lunch, and was caught by the straw hat and the strong shape of the shadow cast by the overhead awning. I saw the scene straightaway as a pastel and made a drawing in my sketch-book.'

▷ *The Striped Umbrella, the Piazza, Venice*

Pastel and watercolour, 9¼ × 4¾in (23.5 × 12.1cm), 1992

An unusual composition with a glimpse of the Ducal Palace sandwiched between the Campanile to the left and Sansovino's Library to the right. The young people on the right are cut by the edge of the picture, and their striped umbrella becomes more important in the composition than they are. In contrast to the firmly handled steps, the pavement of the Piazza is fluid, reflecting the people with their umbrellas. Notice the economical use of pastel with the buff paper beneath playing an important role as a colour in itself.

studio where I have lots of boxes. Each box contains a variety of tones within one colour, a box of grey-blues, browns, tans, yellows, reds, dark greens, light greens, cool whites, warm whites, pale pinks, violets and blues, some still quite sizeable, others tiny pieces. I also have a "new box" for newly bought colours. I work with three or four pastels in my hand and keep those ones I have used or think I will be using in the lids. This helps me to keep some sort of order. I normally use quite a number in one work; I could find myself using as many as twenty.

'Some time ago John Linfield and his wife Monica called in on us. John Linfield, who learnt from John Ward, is a watercolourist whose work I much admire for its audacious scope, charm and vitality. When the two of them visit us, animated conversation has the upper hand, and on this occasion the hem of his jacket caught and distributed the box of blue-greys all over the floor. It was useless for me to say that I had done the same thing many times before; a few days later I received a box with four beautiful pastels, each one a different grey. I decided to return the compliment by sending them a little work done with just those four pastels. In fact I did need one orangey-pink from another box, but working with those four close colours made me wonder why I usually think I need so many to achieve what I want.

'I invariably start a pastel drawing with a CarbOthello pencil. At some stage I should decide whether it shall be foremost a drawing with just a few areas of beautiful pastel to enhance and explain, or the minimum of drawing and mostly pastel. I am very much aware of the real danger of having neither dominate, both taking from the expressiveness of the other, each making the other look overworked. I look at Whistler's pastels and marvel at those that

Corner of San Marco, Venice
Sketch-book drawing, 1992

Aspens by the Log Cabin
CarbOthello pencil on Canson paper, 1993

◁ The Confidential Conversation at Fortnum's
Pastel, 7¾ × 9¼in (19.7 × 23.5cm), 1991

Diana has referred to the circumstances behind this pastel drawing on page 44. Notice the boldness of the composition, which is dominated by the strong pink of the Fortnum and Mason's sofa in the foreground, reflected in the chairs behind. Two ladies on the left are engrossed in their gossip, while the young girl looks directly towards us. Diana is interested in the relationship between the people in her paintings and pastels, and has achieved a marvellous 'character' in the lady with the black and white hat, her teacup poised in her hands. The brilliant white of the table-cloth is set against the bare area of carpet to the right, while our eyes are led past the other diners to the lights in the room beyond. There is also a subtle play on pinks in the difference between the orange-pink of the sofa and the stronger pink of the young girl's scarf.

Diana's pastels are never overworked, and she always achieves a lightness of touch, allowing the paper beneath to show through and become part of the tonal scheme. Her admiration for Whistler's pastels is reflected in the economy of line and detail, and the elegance of her marks.

▷ The Art Institute of Chicago
Pastel, 7 × 8½in (17.8 × 21.5cm), 1992

'I made a number of sketch-book notes of the people looking at the works in several of the rooms in the gallery, and did actually see, for just a moment, the juxtaposition of the lady in black and white against the larger 'gallery goer' in the pink blouse with her black camera. The position of the rope struck me as crucial to the design.'

The Path through the
Aspens
Etching/aquatint, 1991

achieve such elegance of drawing enriched by his perfect placing of the pastel, and in others the richness and luminosity of the pastel with just accents of delicate expressive drawing. His best pastels look inevitable and as if he couldn't do otherwise, but no medium can ever be mastered every time, even by Whistler.

'I find that it is all too easy to add just one more little area of pastel to what I had hoped was to remain mostly a drawing. I find it the most difficult thing in the world to stop. If I've gone too far I can either erase whole areas and begin again with the drawing, and I often do this, or carry on obliterating the drawing with areas of pastel, re-thinking the shapes with the pastel. As with watercolour begun on the basis of a drawing, it seems important to me to re-assess at every stage, never to rely or follow what I have underneath without re-thinking.

'One of the charms of working on a townscape is enjoying the contrast between the static architecture and the organic shapes of the people, dogs, cats or birds. I usually start with the area of the sky, the architecture and the larger areas of light and dark made by the shadowed parts against the sunlit areas. I can then begin to play the organic shapes against this framework. This will probably lead me back again to the architecture, so that before I have gone far, I shall be putting down little connecting touches, and, I've no doubt, completely re-thinking some areas [see *Queuing at the Fenice*, page 107].

'I always intend to use the smooth side of Canson paper, but every now and then I find I have done the initial drawing on the wrong side. The rather mechanical tooth doesn't show up until I start working with the pastel. I am loath to start again, so usually resign myself to the almost pointillist effect of the rough side and try to make use of it. In a way it does have its own particular quality, but as this is rather dominating I don't make a practice of it.

'I mostly choose the middle-toned papers to work on. I keep a stack of voilet-grey and blue-grey in both studios, Kew and Wales. That gives me a choice of warm and cool. Occasionally I come across a rich brown paper which may be too "hot" to work on directly, but with a wash of blue-grey watercolour it makes an attractive alternative for particular works. In the same way that I choose what I think will be an appropriately toned panel for starting an oil, I choose my paper for a pastel with the same kind of thoughts running through my mind. The choice will certainly influence the outcome, as the colour of the paper will play a part, even if I am unwise enough to overload it with pastel.' (See *Tourists in Orvieto*, page 114.)

WATERCOLOURS AND ETCHINGS

'I am not yet at home with watercolour; I need to have exactly the right paper which can take and hold a brush mark, and the brushes I use have to be the best sable in order to have a spring and hold a generous amount of paint. I admire Cézanne's watercolours and relish his build-up of exquisite, meaningful brush marks. When I started to work in watercolour I tried to emulate his approach, but "meaningful" is the operative word, and any attempt to copy the style without understanding the mind behind, ends up as little more than a mannerism. However, the simple approach of adding small touch to small touch, each contributing to describing the forms, did help me to develop a language which has been variously appropriate to the vineyard scenes of France and Italy. Those vineyards seldom fail to seduce me to do something with them in that most beguiling of mediums [see *Tending the Vines*, page 111].

'Above all I admire Turner's watercolours, but if I want to learn from him, I have to become more acquainted with a much more complex language than I have yet explored. I think Leslie Worth is an artist who does understand something of Turner's language and has in a masterly way developed his own, quite individual, poetic approach. Being a member of the Royal Watercolour Society, I do show a number of works at each Members' Exhibition, but there are still too many that don't ever get resolved. Watercolour is not a forgiving medium.'

Diana Armfield also does the occasional etching which includes aquatint, and although she is not trained in the medium, she thinks that it is both useful and fun to work in different techniques. She finds etching exciting when things are going well, but thoroughly frustrating when they are not. Clearly she is not a born etcher! She and Bernard have two presses: a big Victorian example in Kew and one in Wales made by their engineer son, Andrew Dunstan. The press is an innovative design, light enough for a strong woman to carry, but large enough to take good-sized plates. It prints beautifully. Andrew Dunstan makes each press individually in his back yard, along with many other of his inventions. Diana uses mostly copper plates which she finds easier to control than zinc.

◁ *Sun Setting over the Salute, Venice*
Watercolour, 6¼ × 6¼in (15.8 × 15.8cm), 1993

This is one of Diana's favourite scenes, the winter
sun setting over the Santa Maria della Salute seen
from the Piazzetta, but unusually it is painted in
watercolour. The medium helps the artist to create
an image full of light and atmosphere. Notice how
the figures, while accurately depicted, are not
overworked and have a great sense of movement
and life. The artist has obviously enjoyed the
freedom of the medium to create a fluid and
luminous work.

▷ *Queuing at the Fenice, Venice*
Pastel, 11 × 8in (27.9 × 20.3cm), 1988

'I had both looked at this view and drawn it many
times, partly for the pleasure of the lamp-post and
the rosy wall behind, but it was not until I saw it
with the queue of people that I could make
anything of it. The touch of white next to the lady
in black seen against the wall clinched the idea for
me.'

7

REFLECTIONS

(Opposite)
Diana Armfield's studio in Kew, c.1990 (South-facing with Chinese-style blinds to diffuse the sunlight. On dark days there was a daylight tube with a 150W ordinary bulb at either end over the window; in the centre of the room were three more 150W bulbs fixed onto an old breadboard hanging from the ceiling.)

JH: You once remarked to me that you should not put anything into this world which is not, in some way, life-enhancing. What exactly do you mean by this?

DMA: I have always felt that, with the amount of destruction and ugliness created by human events and attitudes, it is one's job, as an artist, to counter this. If you don't counter it, you reflect it, and much of what passes for art at the moment is nothing but a reflection of the disorder in the world.

I see art as a process of ordering. Even the violent works of Goya, Picasso and the German Expressionists create a sense of order, whereas much of what is done today has no sense of order at all. It contributes nothing to life.

Some time ago I was listening to a lecture by Lord Porter. As far as my unscientific mind could grasp, he described the forces of destruction as leading to entropy. He argued that there are two forces at work in the universe: a strong force that returns order back to chaos, and a smaller life force leading to the creation of highly ordered organisms. These forces are clearly differentiated, one on the side of progress, the other on the side of entropy, or the tendency to return the world to dust. I see this as the difference between the death force and the life-giving force which makes us.

JH: People might say that your work is irrelevant to modern life as it really is.

DMA: On the contrary. Art can attempt, in however small a way, to pull back from chaos and destruction. All this sounds pompous, because my work is small and insignificant, but nevertheless, I am trying to show myself and others that there is an order which can be seen in the rhythms and harmonies of the best man-made structures and the natural world. I hope I can remind people that there are still wild roses to look at, and they are deeply satisfying. At least my art does not add to the pollution in the world.

JH: People nevertheless can say that your art is purely commercial and is only available to those who can afford it.

DMA: I disagree. Most modern art cannot be seen by ordinary people; it is often far too large to fit into ordinary houses. My pictures are very much part of ordinary life. More important than just scale, however, is the fact that many ordinary people dislike the work that the 'art establishment' is forcing upon them. In the past Kenneth Clark fostered artists like Henry Moore and John Piper whom the public in general could admire and enjoy, but today the museum curators and the Arts Council promote artists that have no popular following. The truly commercial art world is the world of the Venice Biennale where all the artists are hyped by the media, but unnourishing to the public. In any case I entirely separate the act of painting from any commercial considerations whatever. Some works take months, even years to resolve, others a couple of hours. This is not reflected in the price.

I believe that art should give pleasure at many levels. I send Christmas cards of my work to friends and when I go to Wales I often see them framed and hanging in farmhouses, usually my paintings of flowers. Perhaps they touch a chord, and help people look more closely and more seriously at flowers. Of course there is always the danger that anything that is inherently beautiful is debased commercially and sullied. Hence the theory that to paint flowers is a weak substitute for exploring other sides of life. For me painting is about observing and learning, and I hope the paintings help others to do the same.

JH: Is your work too comfortable? By that maybe I mean the German word *gemütlich* which suggests a bourgeois, unchallenging, even 'cosy' quality.

DMA: That depends on what you want from life. I find life quite sufficiently challenging as it is, and I want to resolve the difficulties of life in my work. The very painting of the pictures is finding resolutions. This is what much of real art is about – celebrating certain aspects of the world and resolving the visual problems inherent in interpreting in paint. There is sometimes a great effort involved in the making of certain works; at other times they develop with a certainty, but in all of them I feel while painting as if I am walking a tightrope. I'm not that talented, so every time I start a new painting, I'm taking on new problems. So, in answer to your question, my paintings are not 'comfortable' as far as I'm concerned.

People do copy my work, and perhaps some of them are only aiming at a certain easy effect, but if so they are simply looking at the results. When I am in the studio, none of this seems relevant. In all other art forms the comment 'They make it look so easy' is laudatory; only in

◁ *Central Park, New York*
Watercolour, 8¼ × 5in (20.9 × 12.7cm), 1992

'These horse-drawn carriages are such a feature that I sat by the roadside making notes from which to develop a watercolour. I succeeded in putting down enough of the carriages as one or another came past, and of the surroundings, but to get the horse looking at all convincing, I went outside the park where they wait in a line standing patiently. Here I could draw the almost stationary animal at leisure and for my watercolour transfer it back into the park.'

▷ *Tending the Vines, Orvieto*
Watercolour, 7½ × 9in (19.1 × 22.9cm), 1992

The artist describes her watercolour technique on page 105. This light and luminous watercolour reveals some influence of Cézanne and his method of building up his 'exquisite meaningful brush marks'. This is a very radiant work, the tall vines changing greens in the sunlight with a glimpse of Orvieto in the distance. Notice how the artist has used CarbOthello pencil to provide contrast of both tone and texture.

painting and only in the last fifty years has the 'art establishment' wanted to see the signs of anxiety, struggle and despair in the actual work. Isn't this a perverted desire?

JH: It is often said that an artist is essentially a very selfish person. Do you agree?

DMA: Probably. Artists have to be totally engrossed in their work in order to achieve anything, and I suppose that the successful artist is by nature obsessive, except perhaps for those who are exceptionally talented. Art is a profession and, like any other creative profession, it demands commitment.

I do get bothered by the charities which are constantly asking for gifts of pictures; what the organizers don't understand is that they're asking for an artist's capital which can run to hundreds, even thousands of pounds. I would prefer to give a straightforward cash donation. How often do doctors or lawyers donate their services to charity? I would suspect once or twice a year at most, yet artists are constantly being asked to donate their work. However, I do have causes dear to my heart – Friends of the Earth and the like and, of course, the Artists' General Benevolent Institution.

JH: There have only been a few husband and wife partnerships amongst painters. This century there have been three such partnerships where both were members of the Royal Academy: Harold and Laura Knight, Ernest and Dod Proctor and yourselves. What are the problems inherent in such a partnership?

DMA: It is important to avoid competition with each other. Marriage is real, painting is real; it would spoil both to play the game of competition. We deliberately attempt not to trespass onto each other's area of subject matter. For example I used to take my students to rehearsals at the Royal College of Music, and did drawings myself, even starting some not very successful oils. However, Bernard has made musical performances very much part of his work and there is a tacit agreement that I should not tread there, except in Venice where I do draw and paint the orchestras in the Piazza. Likewise, Bernard rarely paints flowers, as we both feel that this is 'my' area.

We have different territories while on painting trips. Bernard works seriously in the hotel room, while my work is in the landscape. We might both later work in the town, but it is in Venice that we really find ourselves looking at the same subjects. In the morning we leave the hotel together, but after a few minutes there is an element of 'You carry on; I've seen something here, so I'm staying behind.'

On the whole this arrangement works well, and in many areas we don't have to risk competition because our interests are different. Bernard rarely paints landscapes except in the way of little sketches or the nude in a landscape setting. I have very little desire to paint the nude, which is, of course, one of Bernard's main interests. It is fortunate for both of us that Bernard wants to draw almost every morning wherever we are, and that for him the subject appears inexhaustible. It is lucky too that he has developed his own talent in such a way that the few minutes that I can give him are rewarding rather than frustrating. I've never been tempted to paint nudes largely because when I'm with people I like to give them my attention and talk to them, rather than paint them. I like drawing people if they are unaware of what I'm doing, but I wouldn't want the responsibility of having a model posing for me. This also applies to portraiture.

I only criticize Bernard's work if he specifically asks for comments, although this can be difficult. If I go into his studio and say nothing, he straightaway asks what is wrong with the picture! Bernard is very reticent and tries not to look at my work unless I ask him to. He might then say 'I don't think this area will do', whereas my criticism tends

Behind the Royal Exchange
Oil, 24 × 20in
(61 × 50.8cm), 1988.
Commission from
Reuters.

◁ *Tourists in Orvieto*

Pastel, 8 × 6in (20.3 × 15.2cm), 1992

In addition to painting the landscape around Orvieto, Diana Armfield likes to draw the inhabitants and tourists of this charming Italian hill town. Notice how the buff Canson paper is used in the buildings in shade on the left, while a pink pastel is floated over the paper for the sunlit building on the right. The paper is also visible in the foreground, ensuring that the surface of the drawing remains lively and interesting with its broken colours. In this pastel the artist has used a brush pen as an experiment.

▷ *Lunch at Fortnum's*

Pastel, 7½ × 8in (19.1 × 20.3cm), 1986

'This was one of my first pastels of the scene in Fortnum's, having been greatly impressed by the chef with his glinting silver carving trolley. The waitress was intended to be a portrait of the particular young woman who so charmingly looked after us. I think it has her stance. I tried to mass the darks and play the lights over this massing and, by a shaft of white table-cloth, bring the eye down to the still life of glasses on the foreground table. This was all developed from a drawing done on the spot.'

Exhibition at Browse and Darby, 1993, with William Darby

into a receptive ear if work, galleries or people fail to give satisfaction.

JH: You have said that you do not paint commissioned portraits, but what is your attitude to other types of commissions?

DMA: I do very few commissions, partly because I want to keep independent and partly from nervousness, but I have to admit that I have actually enjoyed each that I have undertaken. First there is the flattery of being asked, and for a few hours I am more than pleased. This is followed by a reaction 'Why have I committed myself?' However, each time I have carefully given the impression that the work may take a long time to achieve, but in practice I set about it immediately, allowing time for failure and, if necessary, a second attempt. Each commission has led me to see and do something different either in subject matter or in scale, and in retrospect I am grateful for having been pushed into widening my experience. The National Trust commissioned me to paint at Powys Castle, at Erddig, near Wrexham, and at Stourhead in Wiltshire where Bernard was making drawings of the interior with a quartet performing. Dudley Dodd received us and gave us a delicious lunch, before I started work drawing the temple by the lake under a misty winter sky. These commissions took me to three properties which I had seen from a distance, but never found the inclination to explore, and I was rewarded by wandering round these splendid places. The commission to paint the Reuters' Building took me into the City on Sundays, something I should never have done otherwise; and I have already discussed the very rewarding Highgrove commission.

to be more specific, commenting on angles, intervals or colour relationships. This reflects our different styles of teaching; I have always been a more specific teacher than Bernard. Needless to say, critical comments are not always welcome!

As soon as we were married we joined our bank accounts, so the financial success of one over the other has never had relevance. Glory is another matter, and I do think it would be hard if only one had all the attention. We have different galleries in London and only in exceptional circumstances do we agree to a joint exhibition. However, the advantages of a common interest, sympathetic informed criticism and encouragement, and genuine, much-needed admiration far outweigh petty stresses. It is of enormous value and enjoyment to toy with ideas and comments together, and to be able to grumble heartily

JH: What role has the Royal Academy played in your life?

DMA: The Academy has always been a part of my life,

first because the yearly submission of three works by my uncle was regarded by our whole family with a certain reverence and anxiety until confirmation of acceptance arrived through the post. As a schoolgirl, whenever I had achieved a better drawing than usual, I dreamed of having a work hung on those august walls; I did not have the temerity to imagine that I should ever be elected a member. I also visited the major winter exhibitions.

Later, when Bernard was elected a member, I was still engaged in textiles, but I accompanied him to various functions, the Private View Day then being a real 'dressed up' occasion, unlike today. We enjoyed the sight of artists and guests in eccentric or extravagant dress. James Fitton and his wife Margaret always made an entrance in some stunning outfits, and I looked forward to locating Margaret Green with Lionel Bulmer amongst the crowd by her splendid hat which had most likely come from the Design School at Walthamstow where she taught. When I started painting, it seemed natural to submit work myself, and I was lucky enough in the very first year to have a drawing of foxgloves accepted. It was sold, although the prospective buyer offered £16 instead of the marked price of £20. The following year two oils were on the walls, and thereafter my three found a place each year. This didn't mean that I ever felt secure, and one of the very real pleasures of being elected a member is to be relieved of the yearly anxiety which I was not good at concealing. I was never able to develop a philosophical attitude to the idea of rejection, and the fact that it didn't happen in no way lessened my apprehension.

After exhibiting regularly for some ten years, I was included on the candidates list, proposed, I think, by Kyffin Williams, the late Tristram Hillier, the late Richard Eurich and Ken Howard. Kyffin's marvellous paintings of the Welsh mountains, coasts and setting suns always exhilarate me. I only met Tristram Hillier as an elderly man of Old World courtesy in which it was difficult to see the daredevil young man he described in his auto-

biography. Richard Eurich, living on the other side of the Forest from Ringwood, I had known for many years, but didn't really appreciate his enormous talent until I saw his memorial exhibition in Southampton in 1994. I had really only enjoyed his Fine Art Society exhibitions revealing his

Study of people on the round sofa, Impressionist Gallery, Metropolitan Museum, New York
Sketch-book drawing, 1989

◁ *The Salute from the Zattere, Venice*
Pastel, 11 × 7½in (27.9 × 19.1cm), 1993

'This is another view that I have drawn several times and until this last occasion failed to see how I could compose it. In reality I had to look down over the parapet of the bridge to see the water, and then up to see the top of the Salute. This could be a recipe for disaster, although easily managed by masters of decorative perspective invention; Rex Whistler comes to mind.'

▷ *Field of Sunflowers near St Félix*
Oil, 13¾ × 17¾in (34.9 × 45.1cm), 1985

Diana often goes to the Aude and Herault districts of France in the late summer to paint the sunflowers, and this is one of the most beautiful examples of her landscapes with sunflowers. The flowers are difficult to paint and she has resisted the temptation to become too precise, suggesting instead a vibrant, moving field of yellow and brown. This sense of movement is accentuated by the S-shape which dominates the composition, taking our eye towards the distant blue hills. The village on the right provides an architectural anchor in the waving sea of sunflowers.

Tourists in Orvieto
Sketch-book drawing for
pastel (page 114), 1992

wonderfully odd and witty beach scenes where he played with the space between beach and horizon.

I must assume that I had enough support to be added to the list, as I received a letter asking for my consent. I don't think I was the only one to assume that having got on the list, election would follow within a couple of years, but it soon became clear that it was very much a first step and that there might never be another. It was a further ten years before that second step was accomplished and it came at the precise time when I had decided that it could never happen. I was far away in another world in my studio, when the phone rang. I heard Bernard's voice through the answerphone message. I had switched on the machine to insulate myself from the outside world; he had slipped out of the General Assembly to tell me the result, and despite the confusion of noise I could hear the good news.

The Academy has changed over the years both as a result of its Presidents and the fact that it has become a great centre for international exhibitions, needing a huge staff of administrators who inevitably run it as a successful business. It is a far cry from the time when the members themselves were the organization as well as an Academy, and a tiny staff, known to all, supported their efforts. However, it is the Schools and Summer Exhibition for which the public and a very large number of professional and semi-professional artists hold the Academy in esteem and affection, and however big the organization becomes, those two functions can only be run by the members themselves, and will therefore, I hope, continue to have that special note that only artists can provide. To be on the Council at the selection and involved with the hanging of the Summer Exhibition is an extraordinary experience, enormously rewarding in the face of so much genuine and inventive talent – and, I have to add, rubbish; but I confess that it is a gruelling time.

JH: The New English Art Club has also played a part in your artistic life.

DMA: The NEAC was my introduction into the world of art societies, and I hold it in great affection. I was just in time to be aware of the generation of Ethelbert White and Vincent Lines – the latter we once met clambering into a train dressed in khaki shorts, rucksack on his back, and pushing his bicycle up through the passenger door. They both had a certain air of unambitious integrity about them, commanding quiet deference from the younger members. By the time I was elected this older generation had gone and the NEAC, though still the best of the societies, was hardly keeping its head above water. Since then the reticent grey-green tendency on the walls of its exhibitions has developed into something of a wider scope, interest and confidence, which reflects more accurately the true and often eccentric character of the members. For a great many years I attended all selection and hanging days, and there were no occasions more animated, more outspoken to the point of shouting, and more fun to be part of. How often do we think that the figures of the past were somehow larger in character than our contemporaries. For once I think the NEAC can boast its share of larger-than-life characters.

JH: I believe that you are a member of several other societies.

DMA: I am a member of too many art societies, but, as each has its own character, I stay with them all. When I was elected to the Royal Watercolour Society it was housed in grand surroundings in Conduit Street and run with great authority by Malcolm Fry. Recently elected members felt both privileged and also very 'new' for quite some time. Now based in the Bankside Gallery under the successive presidencies of Maurice Sheppard, Charles Bartlett and now Leslie Worth, the atmosphere is rather different, with the Society undertaking many educational activities and a much wider variety of work. The Royal West of England Academy is a pleasure with its beautiful galleries and west country feel, where we can meet old friends, among them the erudite George Sweet who takes time from his work to talk about painting, as well as have a good gossip, which is rarer than you might think amongst painters. The Royal Cambrian Academy secures my Welsh connection and I only wish I could give more to it and to the Pastel Society of which I am an honorary member. I have been asked several times to join the Society of Women Artists, but have declined, not for lack of sympathy, but because I cannot help regarding all exclusive groupings whether old, young, black, white, men or women, as divisive and likely to lead to intolerance.

JH: You have been exhibiting at Browse and Darby in Cork Street for many years; can you discuss the relationship between gallery and artist?

DMA: The relationship between gallery and artist is very close and of the utmost importance to both; much more than purely financial considerations are involved. Sometimes I am asked by a collector whether I would welcome a visit to my studio with a view to a direct purchase from me. Of course I am pleased and flattered; I enjoy making the acquaintance of collectors and I like to know where my work is going and what company it will keep. However they sometimes ask what commission the gallery takes. When told, they are sometimes ready to be indignant on the artist's behalf, but most artists know exactly why the commission is high at present and don't like to hear any criticism of their own gallery, in rather the same way that portrait painters will hear no word against their sitters.

The artist provides the work and I like to provide it ready framed, in fact until I see it framed I cannot be certain that I will not want to work over certain passages,

◁ *Aspens along the Path in the Rockies*
Pastel, 9¾ × 10¾in (24.8 × 27.3cm), 1990

This fresh and radiant pastel resulted from one of Diana's visits to her son and daughter-in-law. She finds the Rockies a challenge and quite different to the landscape of Southern France and Italy; she finds the scale of the mountains and the space difficult to interpret, preferring to imply it by glimpses through the aspen or cottonwood trees. In this pastel the great sense of space is suggested by the distant blues of the mountain range beyond and the hint of a vast field of corn stretching towards them. This is contrasted with the vivid blues and greens of the trees and grass in the foreground, which are themselves set off by the white tree trunks. A path winds its way round to the left inviting us to explore the space further.

▷ *Distant View of Orvieto*
Oil, 8½ × 10in (21.5 × 25.4cm), 1991

A 'classic' Armfield landscape full of light, movement, joy and warmth.

nor can I decide whether it is a painting I really want to see in my Browse and Darby show. Having received the work, it is now for the gallery not only to sell it, but to build and confirm the artist's reputation. This must be quite a task when they have perhaps a dozen or more artists to look after. The show, be it every two or three years, is a big event for the artist, and I can't be the only one who needs encouragement and moral support for some time before the exhibition opens. I was lucky enough to be chosen by just the gallery I wanted to be connected with, for I had always felt that one of Browse and Darby's great strengths was to show only those artists whose work they admired. However, one has only to think realistically to know that on their side, they must sometimes watch their artists develop in ways which try them, and a dealer who lacks some depth of tact, diplomacy and even deviousness probably won't keep the same artist for any length of time. As artists we are very alert to the kind of gallery which tries to channel the work in a direction which they know they can sell. Most artists resent any such pushing.

I never work for a show, preferring just to paint according to the energies of the day and then to set on one side whatever I think is a little special, not necessarily an important work, but one which for me has some particular quality or felicity. Every so often I take a batch down to the gallery in preparation for my next show. William Darby and I then go through them together. I expect noises of appreciation, and if a work doesn't exact any, I suggest taking it away for another exhibition. Before the show, the gallery has the responsibility of photographing the work and producing the catalogue.

Many artists and galleries are secretive about their clients and are reluctant to divulge names. I have always held that all names and addresses of customers should be handed over by both, and the more widely distributed the catalogue, the more interest is aroused. Some artists like to be in at their 'hanging', but I like to arrive fresh and

surprised; however, this is really only possible because William Darby is a naturally gifted hanger. Finally there is the private view, the actual selling of the work, collecting the money and the day-to-day response to the public.

When I do have someone to my studio, I invariably enjoy the occasion, but it usually takes the whole morning or afternoon. Seldom does much work get done that day, and I certainly couldn't envisage being my own gallery. It is almost impossible to look someone in the eye and quote them the full price: confidence falters and you hear yourself saying 'Oh well, we'll say such and such.' Your gallery saves you all such embarrassments. Of course the commission is high for the artist, but I am realistic enough to know, however, that this has to do with rates, rent, advertising and taxes rather than gallery policy. There is another category: 'dealers from home', and 'out-of-town galleries'. In their own way they contribute a great deal by the interest they give between shows. They do a wonderfully encouraging and 'buttering-up' job, which I hope is mutual.

JH: For many years you taught in art schools, but you have said that you are out of sympathy with much that is going on there today. What has changed since you first taught and what, in your view, has gone wrong?

DMA: In the past, art courses provided an education which could lead to many different careers. It provided a breadth of approach, discipline and the fundamental craft of painting; many of the courses I taught were very intense. My own teaching was aimed at increasing the students' powers of observation; I tried to open their eyes but never to influence them directly in matters of style or ideas. Most students are easily influenced and it is difficult to avoid 'followers'; it is the 'odd bods' who stick to their guns who act as a leaven in the class. Maurice de Sausmarez tried to dilute the influence of powerful personalities at the Byam Shaw by employing many part-time tutors of very different outlooks. This made lunch time at the local pubs a most stimulating part of the day, as both tutors and students lunched together, crowding round little tables exchanging ideas. Maurice himself was charismatic and so many-sided that both tutors and students could seldom refrain from endlessly discussing his personality. The traditions Maurice started were carried on after he died by Geri Morgan and the school continues to flourish.

Then in the 1960s the emphasis began to shift and everyone started to talk about 'ideas' or attitudes of mind. It was only the old-timers like Rodney Wilkinson, Peter Garrard and myself who discussed fundamentals and ways of observing, as well as the actual act of painting. I had revived the idea that students at the Byam Shaw should prepare their own canvases and boards, but this lapsed and the job was given to a technical assistant. I dare say the old NDD was very dull, but it was also thorough, and it did insist on students acquiring basic knowledge and competence.

This change of attitude was summed up in the Coldstream Report which I considered fatal. It introduced theoretical courses such as 'Basic Design' and 'Colour Theory' but they were not related to observation. Students found my course hard work, but I think fun as well; they were mostly first and second year, and I felt that at least I had sowed certain seeds: in later years I felt some despair because they were only interested in systems and conceptual art. Students were encouraged to have 'an idea' however small and insignificant it might be: I remember one American girl who told me that she was 'zeroing in on the corner of the studio' for the whole term. I feel that 'ideas' should arrive naturally out of the actual practice of painting, life's experience and all the talk that goes on in student years.

I found it more and more difficult to get students to look and observe and we no longer even shared the same language. There is a difference between ideas and concept on the one hand and observation on the other. Observation and drawing can be taught, but I think it is an impertinence to attempt to teach ideas. The Byam Shaw moved to North London, and although I continued to do some teaching on Wimbledon Common, I took the opportunity to give it up. I found teaching most stimulating and enjoyable, and it always made me look at my own work afresh.

There is no lack of talent today, but without direction and discipline talent cannot develop. After the 1960s English art schools in many ways let their students down; the teaching remained much better in the Scottish colleges. There is a need for people to be creative: amateur and evening classes are fuller than ever before, and just as things went wrong in art schools, so adult and leisure classes have flourished; the creative urge is as strong as ever. I am also encouraged by the development of workshops such as the ones run by the Royal Watercolour Society and the newly established New English Art Club School of Drawing. Not only do they provide instruction by professional practising artists, but they also provide figurative artists with the chance of teaching, which has been virtually abolished in the art schools in the old part-time capacity.

JH: Much modern art sets out to shock. I suppose it stems from the desire to be original whatever the cost in artistic quality and integrity. How do you, as a figurative and essentially a traditional artist, cope with this?

DMA: None of this really affects me. I sometimes blow up when I hear about the latest piece of conceptual art which is intended solely to 'shake people's preconceptions', but I don't consider that shocking people is part of art. If you have to shock in order to say something, you are failing. Some modern art is witty: for example Picasso's sculpture which I see as a sort of carnival art. It is clever and witty; I enjoy it, but for me it lacks significance.

Another characteristic of modern art is the need to explain everything in words. I feel that a work of art should not require a written explanation in order to be understood. Painting and conceptual art has become more and more about ideas, and the actual putting down of the idea is often crude and ineffectual. We've really gone back to an earlier period when the idea or message was more important than the work of art itself.

The art establishment – the Arts Council and the 'mafia' of museum curators who run events such as the Venice Biennale and the Turner Prize – is quite out of touch with the concerns of most people. Many of the artists they support could not survive in the commercial world of art, and rely entirely upon other funding.

JH: I know that both you and Bernard are interested in classical music, attending concerts and operas. What role has music played in your life?

DMA: Music has always seemed to me to parallel painting. My mother played the piano and accompanied us for singing and in our attempts at making music. Gramophones were improving in the thirties, and as a child I got to know many works of Bach, Beethoven and above all the Mozart operas; along with dance music, I loved them all. Later on with Andrew at the piano, it was very enjoyable to play some chamber music and I remember Patrick Symons RA bringing his cello to play

with us. I also enjoy singing and for some fifteen years I sang in the University College School Choral Society. Mothers were there to strengthen the alto section, and it was a privilege to be taught many of the great choral works. Any analysis of music could be applied to painting, and the two seem closely linked to natural growth and form. I am one of those who nearly always have music on while I'm in the studio; anything from Bach to Mahler seems right for this, but apart from the Mozart operas and some of the choral works, I find the voice a distraction.

JH: Have any books or authors influenced you?

DMA: D'Arcy Thompson's *Growth and Form*, dealing as it does with the geometry linking all natural forms and forces, was a revelation to me. The book is only a memory: it vanished off our shelves some years ago. We have a whole shelf of John Ruskin and I relish his style and argument, so absolutely right and then totally wrong, even on the same page. All literature is a discipline with forms which correspond to art and music, perhaps at its peak in the great nineteenth- and early twentieth-century novels.

JH: What do you hope for the future?

DMA: Health and long life for all of us, and painting with greater command, richness and certainty of touch.